DREAMING A CITY
FROM WALES TO UKRAINE

With many thanks to Alexandr Kirilenko and the British Council in Donetsk, Steve Groves and BBC Wales, Susan Edwards and the Glamorgan Record Office, members of the Teliesyn co-operative, David Parker, Mike Campbell, Ann Guzhvenko, Helen Groubsky, Orla and Owen Thomas, Lynn and Rosemary Jones, Siân Gale, Gwen Davies, Jo Gower and Y Lolfa.

DREAMING A CITY
FROM WALES TO UKRAINE

Colin Thomas

For Hazel

First impression: 2009

© Colin Thomas, 2009

Published with the financial support of the
Welsh Books Council

Design: Alan Thomas

ISBN: 9781847711243

Printed on acid-free and partly recycled paper
and published and bound in Wales by
Y Lolfa Cyf., Talybont, Ceredigion SY24 5HE
e-mail ylolfa@ylolfa.com
website www.ylolfa.com
tel 01970 832 304
fax 832 782

PROLOGUE – DAY DREAMING

Enter the dream-house, brothers and sisters,
                                              leaving
Your debts asleep, your history at the door:
This is the home for heroes, and this loving
Darkness a fur you can afford….

This is a book about a city that invented and re-invented itself three times. Each of its names – Hughesovka, Stalino and Donetsk – represented the dream of a fresh start, a new beginning.

John Hughes, born and brought up in Merthyr as a working man under the control of an all-powerful local family, dreamed of creating from nothing a mighty industrial city with no-one but himself and his family in charge. In 1917, the best of the Communists dreamed of taking over what the Hughes family had built and turning it into the 'city of steel', a city run by and for its own workers. And, when by 1961 the Soviet Communist Party had acknowledged the terrible things that had been done by Stalin in the name of Communism, it aimed at a fresh start and dreamed of a 'city of roses'. They believed that it would be possible to turn an industrial city into a thing of beauty.

So an account of this city tells a bigger story.

It tells the story of Russia, Ukraine and the Soviet Union over the last 150 years in microcosm. But it also says something about dreams and dreamers, and whether hopes for a better world are ever achievable.

At Cathays Grammar School in Cardiff, I was often accused of day dreaming, and had to admit that my teachers had a point. When the tedium of the classroom became too much to bear, I knew I had only to look out of the window and into the distance to drift away into another world. A shout or a clip across the ear would bring me back to my desk and I wanted to respond – 'Well, what's so wrong with dreaming?'

A career in film-making was perhaps the inevitable outcome, though television turned out to be less of a dream factory than I had envisaged. It was only in that heady year of 1968 that I became vividly aware of fellow dreamers, of others both inside and outside the media who believed in the possibility of turning dreams into reality.

I first heard about Gwyn Alf Williams, whose ghost walks through the pages of this book, through the History Workshop movement. Founded by a group of socialist historians and worker-students from Ruskin College, Oxford, it set out to free history from the grip of academia. Its manifesto proclaimed that "history should become common property, capable of shaping people's understanding of themselves and the society in which they live."[1]

Gwyn spoke at one its early conferences and then wrote up his talk for an article in its first journal.

It described the journeys of the Welshmen who went in search of a tribe of Welsh-speaking native Americans, Red Indians as they were once called, who were thought to be descendants of Prince Madoc. The tribe did not exist but the claim had a huge impact back in Wales – as did his article on me. It was partly the combination of dazzling scholarship with pungent wit – the sentence "Life gets *tasteless,* don't it?"[2] pops up in the middle of a careful disentangling of fact from fiction – but it was also his plethora of challenging ideas. Dreams, he convincingly demonstrated, even those dreams without a scintilla of truth in them, could change the way a nation thought.

My first meeting with Gwyn was in 1981. He was then in his last year as Professor of History at University College Cardiff, and for the next fourteen years we shared a dream, making thirty television programmes together. It was no coincidence that I met Gwyn in the year in which my father died, so in retrospect I can see that he became something of a father figure. But consciously it was with his inspirationally-hopeful side that I identified, the notion that dreams could not only be eloquently articulated but could actually be achieved.

Soon after meeting, we made *The Dragon Has Two Tongues*, a thirteen-part series on the history of Wales for HTV Wales and Channel 4. Gwyn joined the Teliesyn production company, a Cardiff based co-operative of which I was a founder member. We aspired not only to make challenging programmes

but also to make them in a way that challenged the BBC/ITV assumptions about rigid hierarchies. In Teliesyn, we wanted all members to be able to share in decision making about the company: production assistants as well as producers, sound recordists as well as directors, and if we made a profit, it would be shared equally between all members.

The original proposal for a Hughesovka/Stalino/Donetsk series of programmes was submitted via Teliesyn. We couldn't get either HTV or BBC Wales interested and it was only when we offered it to BBC network that we got a positive response. BBC Two network could see our argument that the story of this one town told a wider story. The series *Hughesovka and the New Russia* won Best Documentary at the first BAFTA Cymru awards ceremony in 1991 which was transmitted live on Welsh television. When Gwyn began to walk back to the Teliesyn table he noticed that the HTV and BBC Wales executives who had turned the proposal down were energetically applauding him. To the bafflement of viewers at home, he took one hand away from the precious trophy and gave them a vigorous V-sign.

In writing a book about the city that became Donetsk, I have found it impossible to detach that story from that of my friendship with Gwyn and from my own aspirations as a film-maker. In *The Dragon Has Two Tongues,* the differing interpretations of Welsh history offered by Gwyn and Wynford Vaughan Thomas were built into the structure of the series and we tried to continue that approach after

Wynford's death, with historical figures sometimes challenging the interpretation of their life that Gwyn was offering. So I will try to be honest not only about a perspective on the city that he and I shared but also about our sometimes sharp disagreements. Just occasionally that V-sign of his was waved in my direction too.

What has become of the Donetsk dream now? In 1991, it was possible to split the programmes neatly according to its name changes. But since then the town has re-invented itself yet again and become part of Ukraine. I realised that I would have to go back there and see if the dream of a changed city had come closer than the earlier attempts to being achieved. The place was now becoming something of an obsession and in 2007 I wrote a radio play called *Hiraeth in Hughesovka* set in the town, subsequently broadcast on Radio 4. In it the protagonist David Protheroe asks his Ukrainian girlfriend Anna Penkova how she felt about the building excitement in the city in 1917 that the world may be about to be turned upside down. She answers "I'm thrilled by it," then hesitantly, "but frightened too."

I anticipated encountering both responses when I made the arrangements for a return visit in spring 2008, after fifteen years away. Russia had just threatened to point its missiles towards Ukraine because the latter planned to join NATO. Was the city waking up from a dream – or entering a nightmare?

…Grow nearer home – and out of the dream-
house stumbling
One night into a strangling air and the flung
Rags of children and thunder of stone niagaras
tumbling,
You'll know you slept too long.

Cecil Day-Lewis, "Newsreel"

CHAPTER ONE – MUD AND BULLOCK CARTS

Flame and smoke all around you, molten iron trickling at your feet, warning shouts from the men opening the blast furnace. This was John Hughes's first day at Cyfarthfa ironworks where, tradition has it, he learnt his trade from his engineer father. It must have been a terrifying one.

I have tried to convey on screen what those ironworks were like by filming at Blackwood in the most primitive Welsh foundry I could find – when Michele Ryan the producer turned up, she was appalled and said she would have stopped the filming had she realized what conditions were like. Having now attended film Health and Safety courses myself, I can see her point. But filming that day gave me an insight into John Hughes's apprenticeship. One of the workers clutched the hook of an overhead crane and was dangling by one hand as he hitched a lift over a stream of molten metal. "Safety glasses? No, we don't bother with them," the foreman told me – I couldn't help noticing he only had one eye.

Just to hold your own in an environment like this required remarkable toughness and John Hughes clearly had it. According to a letter in the 21 July 1900 edition of the *Merthyr Express*, he was born in Merthyr in 1815, either at Penydarren or Caepantywyll. Merthyr was a very tough town. Slums like 'China' were seen as no-go areas by the local authorities and proud Merthyr man Gwyn Williams acknowledged that at that time "public order was certainly precarious."[3] John Hughes would have been just sixteen at the time of the Merthyr Rising, which ended with the wounding of seventy men, the killing of twenty-five and the hanging of one – Dic Penderyn. Dic is still remembered in a bilingual memorial plaque on the wall of the Central Library, Merthyr Tydfil – "Martyr of the Welsh Working Class".

Whether John Hughes would have seen Dic Penderyn in that way is another matter; from the outset he seems to have been a company man. Visiting Hughes's first workplace today, it's difficult to imagine it in its heyday. Then, it was the largest ironworks in the world, producing 13,000 tons of iron a year; now it is desolate and, when I walked up to the Cyfarthfa site on a winter's day, there were just two people there, a bored security man and a technician, checking for asbestos before industrial archaeologists completed their last survey of the site. As the rain turned to snow, I sheltered in the cathedral-like arch that once bridged the gap between the seven massive blast furnaces, almost all that survives of the 'glowing mountain', the 'great wonder' that had so impressed George Borrow on his tour of Wales.

The trees now prevent you from seeing the castle which Hughes's employer, William Crawshay the second, had built for himself. But Penry Williams's magnificent painting of the puddling furnaces and rolling mills at night makes it clear that Crawshay's workers would certainly have seen it then. Perhaps that is where John Hughes's dream began; his fellow workers must have resented that display of opulence on the hill above them but maybe it was here that the apprentice iron worker decided that one day he would be up there, looking down on his own workforce.

Cyfarthfa Ironworks Interior at Night by Penry Williams 1825.
Courtesy of: Cyfarthfa Castle Museum and Art Gallery

After Cyfarthfa, John Hughes worked at Ebbw Vale and then moved on to Uskside Engineering Works in Newport in the early 1840s. He was clearly rising fast in the hierarchy and by the time he was

twenty-five, he had become what the authors of that Merthyr plaque would have considered to be a member of the capitalist class. He took over the works in Newport and developed it into a foundry specialising in anchors and chains for ships.

I recently walked along the banks of the Usk in Newport, period map in hand, hoping to find a battered relic of John Hughes's works, if anything at all. To my surprise I found an engineering factory still functioning on the same site, part of it still referred to as the 'arms shop', even though it hasn't produced armaments for many years. One of its workers showed me the railway lines that once carried iron ore into the works and brought the finished product out. "Until recently we still ran a truck along it to carry the heavy stuff but the management here were too bog-eyed to realize how useful it was and sold it for scrap."

He stepped outside and pointed out to me where the Tredegar Arms had stood, demolished just a decade or so ago. It once supplied beer to the workers at Uskside Engineering and it is here that John Hughes must have spotted Elizabeth Lewis whose family owned the pub. By 1844 they had married and set up home in Church Street, the road that connected the pub to the works. Hughes's paternal productivity was as impressive as that of his foundry – by 1858 he had a family of eight children, six boys and two girls.

Meanwhile he was developing a range of new products, not only colliery engines and winding gear, much in demand in south Wales at the time, but also his own armament and armour-plating inventions. It looks as if he was then talent spotted by a firm specialising in the arms industry – the Millwall Engineering and Shipbuilding Company. In 1860 he took a seat on the company's Board of Directors.

All that remains of the company now is the skeleton of the dry dock at Burrell's Wharf near the Thames and the walls of what was once the works forge. Behind those walls I saw men at work on *The Forge, 128 stunning studio contemporary style apartments.* The flats, the estate agent's billed, "brings together history and modernity." No other sign now of a site that once employed between 4000 and 5000 men and whose shipbuilding capacity, according to the Survey of London, exceeded that of the Admiralty's dockyard.

By the time he had moved there, John Hughes had acquired a particular expertise in the armaments industry, or defence industry as it prefers to call itself now. Insofar as Hughes was helping to devise ways in which the wooden ships of the Royal Naval could acquire a metal protective shield and so become 'iron-clad', it could be argued that the role was indeed defensive. But the argument is difficult to sustain when he moved into developing new mountings for the heavy naval guns.

Not that John Hughes would have been much bothered by such fine distinctions. The main objective of his company was making money and the success of Hughes's innovations in Admiralty tests at

Portsmouth in 1864, notably his "Millwall shield", no doubt helped to ensure his elevation in the Company. He became its Managing Director, and E. G. Bowen claims that at this point "the reputation of John Hughes and his works as manufacturers of armaments spread far and wide among the nations of the world."[4]

For those without moral qualms, it was a good time to be dealing in arms. Prussia was expanding and turning itself into Germany by attacking first Denmark then Austria; France was strengthening itself against the possibility of a Prussian attack and Russia was busy suppressing yet another Polish revolt. The Russian navy began building what was to become the famous naval fortress at Kronstadt near St. Petersburg and sent over two engineers to Millwall, General Tomieben and Colonel Gern, to supervise the construction of the armaments they required for Kronstadt.

Unsurprisingly, their conversations with Hughes got on to railways – south Wales ironworks like those at Ebbw Vale and Cyfarthfa were the main producers of iron rails throughout the world and Hughes had worked at both. Russia had been embarrassed by how long it had taken to transport troops to the Crimean War and, as Prof. Friedgut puts it in his massive study *Iuzovka and Revolution*, "The railroad was seen as key to the efficient conquest of Russia's vast expanses."[5] Who better to cast that key than the man from Merthyr?

At that time, there was fewer than a thousand

John Hughes, the founder of Hughesovka. Courtesy of: Glamorgan Record Office

miles of railroad in the whole of Russia and, even though the Czarist government realized that the Donetsk area was rich in both coal and iron ore, they had failed to get Russian investors to exploit them. Clearly intrigued by what the Russian engineers had told him, Hughes went to see for himself and was guided around possible sites by a local shepherd. He liked what he saw and seized the chance to buy the rights granted to a Russian prince, Prince Kochubei, to build a rail rolling factory in the area. It cost him £24,000 and very soon afterwards, Hughes did a deal with the Russian government to set up 'the New Russia Company'.

Hughes now chose his site. It was to be one thousand miles away from his homeland and seventy kilometres from the nearest ports, "in the middle of nothing, the steppes of the Ukraine in the Donetsk basin", as Gwyn A. Williams put it in his piece to camera for *Hughesovka and the New Russia*. 'The Ukraine' was how this vast territory was once referred to, literally 'The Borderland' in Russian: as its inhabitants grew more aware of its nationhood, they became more insistent that it should be designated like any other nation – simply as 'Ukraine'.

We spent much of one filming day in 1990 searching for some empty steppe near Donetsk for Gwyn to deliver the line he had prepared. From the Trans-Siberian Railway I have seen mile after mile of steppe stretching into the infinite distance but the Donetsk basin is now so built up that we couldn't find anywhere halfway convincing. At last, with the evening beginning to close in, I spotted somewhere, near the side of the road, that we could just about frame him without a building in shot. He delivered it with his usual passion, his arms spread out, silhouetted against the setting sun, concluding, "An empty land – a furnace in summer, a deep freeze in winter. No country for brass monkeys."

Why on earth did Hughes go? What was the appeal for a fifty-four year old, well-off, happily-married, much-respected businessman to uproot himself and go and live in a shepherd's cottage, while working day and night to set up his plant and mines? Gwyn A. thought it was the adventurer in him, a touch of the gypsy spirit. Soviet historians had a more down to earth explanation – profit. But he already had plenty of that and Professor Friedgut thinks that the motivation was more complex, listing technical challenge, independence and "an additional, more egotistical, motivation".[6]

That motivation, suggests Friedgut, was no less than the founding of a dynasty. In Merthyr he had been at the base of a hierarchy at whose summit was the 'Crawshay Dynasty' who actually called one another 'Majesty' and 'Viceroy'. In London, his accent would have made his working class origins obvious; in the Ukrainian steppe, who would know? And how could his board of directors, most of them in London, challenge him if he chose to set up a company town like the one he had grown up in back home?

The Russian government arrived at an agreement with Hughes that his company would develop coal mining, iron and rail production, and build a branch railway to link with the Kharkov-Azov line. This was then confirmed with the Czar on 16 April 1869 and Hughes returned to London to raise the capital of £300,000 that he needed. The New Russia Company was launched on 3 July 1869 with 6000 shares of £50 each and, with well-known capitalists of the day pitching in, Hughes had no difficulty in raising the cash he needed.

Next he needed workers and who better than the Welsh workers he knew had the necessary skills? From Hughes's point of view, it was a good time to recruit, for the prosperity of the Welsh ironworks was now in decline. Desperate for work, thousands of Welsh men and their families were prepared to uproot themselves and emigrate. The *Merthyr Guardian* for 1869 estimated that as many as a thousand iron workers were prepared to leave the town the following spring.[7] So, when Hughes sailed for the Ukraine in the summer of 1870 with eight shiploads of equipment, he doesn't seem to have had too much difficulty finding and taking with him the seventy or so specialist miners and iron workers he needed.

The journey through the Mediterranean then on to the Black Sea, the Sea of Azov and into the port of Taganrog, was no problem – construction materials were free from import duty in order to provide an incentive to the company. But then those materials had to be dragged across the steppe tracks by bullocks, as roads to what was to become Hughesovka were non-existent. The pioneers arrived at the beginning of an especially grim winter.

I have filmed in what was the Soviet Union in mid winter so have some conception of what it is like to work outdoors at minus zero temperatures: no matter how much you wrap up, the cold eats into any part of your face you leave exposed. How much worse it must have been for Hughes and his men. They recruited some local cossacks and peasants to build the first blast furnace but these were men with no experience of industrial construction. To make matters worse, there was an outbreak of cholera which led to the deaths of some of the Russian and Welsh workers, and the quick exit of others. Hughes, also wrestling with the sluggish local bureaucracy, knew that he was up against it – the concession on import duty from the Russian government was on condition that he not only met a fixed starting date but also quickly achieved the agreed minimum production levels for the mines and furnaces.

In May 1870 the Foreign Office in London received a confidential report referring to the concession that had been granted to "Mr Hughes – an Englishman of the working class" and saying that the Czar had expressed his confidence that the area's mines would be "destined to supply the whole of Russia with coals and iron material."[8] But at that time the entire population of the new town consisted of just 42 families, 164 people – and a herd of 2500

A bullock train hauling a boiler to Hughesovka. Courtesy of: Glamorgan Record Office

bullocks for hauling in the coal, ore and limestone. Internal Russian reports noted that Hughes "energetically supervise[d] the work from morning to evening," backed up by his skilled Welsh workers without whom "it would have been impossible to think that he would have been able to fulfil the obligation he had undertaken."[9]

Nevertheless, Hughes was forced to ask for an extension of his deadline of November 1870. The first blast furnace was completed on 24 April 1871, nine months after construction had begun. But after three days it had to be closed down because of a serious technical problem, caused by faulty materials and the flawed charging of his furnace. As the winter snow melted away, it looked as though the ambitious plans of the New Russia Company were going to be mired just like many of those of the old Russia companies – in mud and bureaucracy.

CHAPTER TWO – ICY WINDS IN THE BLAST FURNACE

Tensions between Welsh and Russian workers cannot have helped, as Hughes and his employees struggled to sort out their problems with the first blast furnace. Evan Williams, who arrived in Ukraine in 1871, regarded the Russians and Ukrainians with an attitude near to contempt: "close to they smelled pretty strongly; in addition they were inveterate thieves." He spoke well of the company that employed him but commented that the Russians "lived like animals in houses dug out of the earth," and giving Williams the impression "that they had never had a wash in their lives."[10]

John Hughes, too, had a low opinion of them, claiming that a British worker outproduced the Russian by a factor of two or three, though he acknowledged that this was because Russian workers had not yet acquired sufficient habits of working.[11] Nevertheless he and his right-hand man, John John from Merthyr, had to make do with those they had employed on the spot. Few of the Welsh migrants seem to have learnt much Russian though Hughes himself spoke some and is said to have signed Russian documents 'I-O3', an approximation to the Cyrillic transcription of his name.[12]

Frantic work on rebuilding the blast furnace enabled the company to try another test firing by November 1871, and two months later Hughes was able to send an exultant telegram to the Russian Minister of Finance: "On Saturday January 22nd the blast furnace began working. Everything going well."[13] A year later the first iron rails were successfully rolled and a second furnace was up and running by 1876. The New Russia Company had even set up its own brickworks to supply the building and furnace-lining bricks that it urgently needed. John John now became the manager of New Russia blast furnaces and, when he eventually returned home after thirty-five years in Hughesovka, was known in Merthyr as 'John John Russia'.

When Gwyn Williams and I went to visit the site in 1988, we were astonished to find that the walls of the furnaces and factory constructed by Hughes and his team were not only still there but were still the walls of part of the works today. It seemed to confirm Professor Friedgut's view of Hughes – a man creating a dynasty, building to last. "His dominant position is attested to by the fact both in journalistic and folk references, the factory was not generally referred to as the New Russia Co. factory, but as *Iuzovskii zavod* – the Hughes factory – and ultimately the settlement around the factory and the mines became officially known as Iuzovka, just as his neighbours' estates bore their family names."[14] Insofar as the Hughes family had social contacts with its neighbours, these would have been mainly with Russian landowners. Such men looked down on

The Hughes family and friends. John Hughes is in the centre at the back and his sons sit on the steps – John James, bottom right, Arthur next to him and Ivor behind John James. Courtesy of: Glamorgan Record Office

the Russian migrant workers who came in search of jobs, as did the local Ukrainian peasantry who tended to see the mining settlements as both ethically and ethnically foreign.

Gwyn and I shared a schoolboyish enthusiasm for steam engines and seized on the idea of a steam train as a visual metaphor for Hughes's drive and energy. We filmed one in 1990 in Caerphilly and I wince now at my lack of awareness of health and safety as the cameraman and I clung to the front of the engine, Gwyn in the driver's cabin, as it chugged back and fore. But historically we were spot on: Hughes is credited with making improvements in the mechanism of the steam engine and by 1876 there were twenty-two steam-powered engines on the Hughesovka site.

Even more impressively, seven coal seams were in operation by then, feeding not only the steam trains on the local lines but also the twelve coke ovens on the site. The iron smelting operation was producing 16,200 tons a year and the complex employed some 2000 people. Most of them were Russian or Ukrainian but the British – mainly Welsh – pioneers tended to dominate the senior jobs. Hughes wrote to Count Valuev, the Russian Minister of State Domains: "When I commenced these works I set my mind upon training the Russian workmen (knowing at the time that it would cost much time and money) with a view to creating a colony of iron-workers who would be attached to the place, and the Directors in London quite approved of my plan."

But he claimed to have been disappointed: "To attain this was my pride and ambition and it is discouraging that the results have not been satisfactory after twelve months experience."[15] His attitude may have been influenced by two strikes in 1874, the year in which he wrote to the minister. The first was by a group of Russian iron workers resisting the introduction of piecework rates, and was soon settled.

The second, by Hughes's mainly Russian coal miners, was more serious. In order to discourage miners, many from peasant backgrounds, from going off to the fields in the summer months, wages were lifted in April and then lowered in October when plenty of workers were available. But Hughes wanted his miners to sign a three-year contract and he deferred paying the increased summer rate in order to pressure them into signing. One hundred and fifty of the 1500 miners responded by going on strike and an almighty row erupted between the miners trying to widen support for their strike, and the factory workers who remained in work. Miners tried to invade the factory but were driven out and fights ended with the factory workers driving out the miners and handing them over to the police.

A year later there was another strike, this time involving factory hands as well as miners. They were indignant that they weren't getting their wages in time for their Easter holiday shopping. Hughes, perhaps revealing his puritan Welsh roots, responded by saying that he had held back the workers' wages for their own good, to prevent them from drinking away their money on the eve of the Easter holiday. Not surprisingly there was a riot directed at local shops and bars rather than at the factory, and the cry went up, "*Ni nam, ni im!*" ("If we can't have the money, neither shall they!")

It seems as if there was an element of playing for time in Hughes's provocative response. In its early years, the New Russia Company often ran into financial crises and it wasn't until the company doctor, Dr. Goldgardt, reassured the angry workers that the money would be telegraphed from St. Petersburg within three days, that both riot and strike came to an end. The local police commander had arrested twenty of the rioting workers but advised Hughes to gather the entire work force together and tell them that from then on they would receive their wages monthly. He took that advice and it helped to produce a long period of industrial calm.

By 1876 Hughes was able to write confidently to the Minister of State Domains that he could achieve his weekly target of one hundred tons of pig iron every day, "the Russian workmen having now become well trained to our system of working." He then added the heavy hint: "We now only want a sufficiency of orders to keep the works fully employed."[16]

He had had those orders, mainly for railway lines, from the outset but a third of the lines were rejected as being below standard. The rejection rate was reduced to ten per cent by 1874 and to five per

The fire brigade of the New Russia Company. Courtesy of: Glamorgan Record Office

cent by 1876 and it seemed as if Hughes had got himself virtually a licence to print money. Then came a body blow: the Russian government, Hughes's main client, decided to change from iron lines to steel, and the New Russia Company had to make a rapid switch from iron to steel production.

Though now sixty-one, Hughes seems to have relished the challenge. He knew that his economic power created resentment amongst some Russian entrepreneurs but he had brought with him an expertise that few of his rivals could match. He was already familiar with the two main methods of steel production from their use in south Wales – the Bessemer process in Dowlais, Ebbw Vale, Blaenafon and Rhymney and the newer Siemens-Martin process at Landore. Perhaps because he had seen the Bessemer 'converters' throwing off showers of sparks when a child – and was conscious of the danger to the wooden houses in the centre of Hughesovka – Hughes opted for the Siemens-Martin method.[17] For a time it seemed as if the quality of the local ore was not up to the standard required for steel rails, and technical hitches briefly led to production sinking almost to zero in 1880. But by 1884 Hughes had three Siemens-Martin blast furnaces in operation producing 20,000 tons of steel a year. The Russian engineer Lebedev, continuing to keep a watchful eye on Hughes and Hughesovka, telegrammed to say, "The question of production of steel rails from local ore may be considered solved."[18]

As Gwyn Williams and I walked through Hughes's town for the first time in March 1988, it was easy to imagine Hughes himself taking just such a stroll a hundred years earlier – and glowing with pride at his achievement. Many of the houses he built, set out in orderly lines with access lanes for the emptying of outhouse receptacles, were still there, and Hughes could have pointed out the twelve-bed hospital, schools, bath-houses, tea rooms, fire brigade and the two churches (one Anglican, the other Orthodox) that he had provided by the late 1880s. Gwyn the Marxist had to admit to a certain grudging admiration for the old capitalist who, in the last years of his life, was enjoying a Crawshay-like lifestyle, including the racing and breeding of horses.

But Gwyn and I were both keen to look at what life was like for those at the hierarchy's base. Not bad, if you were one of the Welsh workers who moved to Hughesovka on the three year contracts offered by the company. It paid for your own passage out and advanced money for your family's too, plus any new clothes or equipment you needed. Skilled workers were paid five roubles a day and in 1880 William Lewis, who became a foreman in Hughesovka, agreed to a piece rate of twelve pounds and threepence for each ton of rail he produced. This enabled him to save enough to buy a house in Cardiff on his return home and, for some years, to live on the income from his savings.

For pay rates like that, men were prepared to put up with the tough conditions in Hughesovka. "I have seen 60 degrees of frost here" wrote Rees Richards, a furnaceman from Dowlais in a letter home in 1889. "I have seen the glass water gauges frozen up. Just fancy. Puddlers… working [at the furnaces] with their gloves on and sheepskin coats on their backs."[19] Reg Taylor of Blaenafon told Gwyn and I about his grandfather's memory of the place: "Very, very rough. Beautiful country in the summer, mind – black grapes would grow in the garden and they had plenty of those. In the winter, the wolves would come to the door and that was it – double shutters on the window, very, very cold."[20]

How much more difficult it must have been to bear that intense cold if you lived in one of the dug-outs inhabited by the Russian workers. E. G. Bowen quotes a description of conditions by one such workman who came to Hughesovka in 1882: "The walls were of stone without plaster of any kind, the roof was made of reeds and the floor was bare earth. Single men slept on common plank beds perhaps fifty or sixty of them in tiers. Workers with families were given one room, no matter how many children they had, and there was a common kitchen with a fire place and coal stove for six families."[21] Faced with conditions like this, most of the Russian migrant miners decided to leave their families in the villages they had come from: an 1884 survey of twetnty-six mining communities in the area revealed that men outnumbered women by six to one.[22]

The part of town where the Russians lived was known as 'The Kennels' ('Sobachevka') or 'Shanghai', a notoriously overcrowded city at the time. While some of the Welsh regarded the Russians with contempt, others, like Rees Richards, looked on them almost with wonderment. In a letter home he wrote: "They are a very hard race of people the natives, they live very plain. The eat nothing but rye bread… Give the natives a lump of bread and a pint of vodka and he is landed."[23]

Many of the Welsh men in Hughesovka came from Merthyr, which had a hard drinking culture of its own. It seems that some of the new arrivals took to Russian ways with enthusiasm, and local industrialist Auerbach wrote that the Welsh "had their own morals and customs… From the Russians they took only one thing, the Russian cursing and the drinking of vodka, which was so much to their taste and which they so misused that Hughes had to send many of them home."[24] Whether they reverted to getting drunk on beer once they got back to Wales is not recorded.

Even if they were able to sink a few vodkas together, the huge disparity between the pay rates of the Welsh and Russians would have prevented the development of any sort of class solidarity. While many of the skilled Welsh workers were on five roubles a day, Russian labourers got just forty kopeks and Hughes's rigorous system of fines meant that those labourers could lose as much as the equivalent of three months wages. There were twenty-eight good conduct rules, including one banning singing and whistling. A worker's day at the factory began at 5.30 a.m. but if he arrived after 5.45, he lost a day's pay, yet still had to put in a day's work. Missing a day's work without cause meant a fine of three days' wages.

No wonder a local Russian newspaper wrote "One must have an entire mountain of afflictions, one must be entirely desperate, one must be in a situation of choosing between life and death to accept the conditions of the Hughes factory."[25] Hughes could argue that the fines went not to him but to a workers' council which distributed the money for the needs of workers' families, and that without strong discipline his Russian workers would have been unable to make the transition to the work-pattern that heavy industry demanded.

Hardly surprisingly, all Hughes's instincts were conservative and individualistic. He, like most Donbass industrialists, did not participate in the first accident compensation fund set up by the Congress of Mining Industrialists in 1884. When he visited Merthyr in 1886, he sounded off about his fellow countrymen: "They tell me the Welsh are all Radicals. I'm not very surprised at it. They don't know better… Send a hundred of the hottest of them to Russia, and I'll guarantee that when they visit their friends for their annual holiday they will say that Beaconsfield" [the former Benjamin Disraeli, Prime Minister in the 1870s] "was the wisest statesman and the greatest England ever saw."[26]

Welsh radicals would have been watching intently the growing ferment in Russia. Czar Alexander the Second had been assassinated in 1881

The Hughes' house in Hughesovka.
Courtesy of: Glamorgan Record Office

by an anarchist group led by a Ukrainian, and in 1887 striking miners from the Rutchenko mines, close to Hughesovka, descended on the town in another attempt to win the support of the workers at the main New Russia factory. Whatever sympathy there may have been for them, Arthur Hughes, one of John Hughes's sons, rallied enough of his men to drive them out, killing three miners in doing so.

John Hughes had received the present of a diamond studded thumb ring from the new Czar, Nicholas II, and was staying at the Hotel Angleterre in St. Petersburg, negotiating the sale of Hughesovka pig iron, when he died on 17 June 1889 at seventy-five years old. There were glowing tributes to him both in Wales and in Russia. "He was a man of great energy and mental resources," wrote the *Merthyr Express*. The St. Petersburg paper *Novosti I Birzhevaia*

Gazeta claimed that "English by origin, he was Russian in his soul, and we may boldly say that he desired Russia's industrial success as passionately as any Russian."

It is hard not to be impressed by what this powerhouse of a man achieved. Whether miners in their hovels, or factory workers losing a day's pay for being fifteen minutes late for work, would have felt quite as enthusiastic as the newspapers' obituary writers is another matter. Imitating the lifestyle of the Crawshay family, he surely aroused much the same response as that felt by workers to the boss in the castle back in Merthyr – some respect but also considerable resentment.

On John Hughes Senior's death, the New Russia Company was now taken over by his four surviving sons, who lived in Hughesovka and already held important management positions in the company. Business was booming but Russia and the Ukraine were moving into a tense and difficult time. The new managing director was John James Hughes, the eldest son. He would soon discover that Hughes Senior's cheerful prescription for averting labour unrest – "Give the men plenty of work!"[27] – which he had inherited from his own father, would prove more and more difficult to deliver.

CHAPTER THREE – SLOW APPROACH OF THUNDER

Although Hughesovka was in Ukraine, most of the miners and many of the factory workers were Russians who had moved south to gain higher wages than they had received as agricultural workers. The slightly-better off Ukrainian peasants looked down on the Russians, especially the miners, seeing them as "filthy unthinkable creatures who knew neither God nor truth and in a dark place were capable of killing a man for a few pennies,"[28] as a contemporary account put it.

The Russian workers in turn focused their contempt on another racial group in Hughesovka – the Jews. The historian Orlando Figes points out that, while Germany and Austria were dismantling their anti-Semitic legislation, the Russian government was adding to theirs, with the new Czar, Nicholas II, interpreting pogroms as acts of patriotism and loyalty.[29] A local police chief expressed the view that "Jews, as has been expressed often in previous surveys, do not belong to the general Russian family. It is senseless to expect loyalty from them."[30]

Not that the Russians in Hughesovka needed much encouragement from on high – throughout Europe Jews had always been a convenient scapegoat for any problem that arose. When Gwyn Williams was researching in 1990 on what happened to the town a century earlier, I know he hoped to find signs of the emerging socialist ideas that were becoming apparent back home in Wales. There were precious few such signs and his voice-over for that section of the film admitted, "these workers didn't often shout 'Workers of the World Unite'; what they shouted was 'Kill the Yids'".

This was the cry that, defying all logic, echoed through the streets during the cholera riots of 1892. Five hundred and twenty-four New Russia workers fell ill and two hundred and thirty-four of these eventually died.[31] Doctors at first tried to isolate the victims in the barracks but this intensified suspicions. Rumours then spread that they were being taken to the town's hospital to be killed off. At first the mob looted only the Jewish shops but Welsh and British workers felt themselves at risk too. Valerie Wood from Cardiff told Gwyn and I that her grandmother had to hide in a truck in the railway sidings overnight to keep away from the trouble.

The Hughes' sons called in a force notorious for its brutality. Peggy Hart recalled her mother telling her that "the whole local population would rush into their houses when they heard the Cossacks coming. They heard the thundering of the horses and the whoops and the Cossacks would come racing along the unpaved streets, wielding their sabres and scattering pigs and chickens right and left."[32] Russian even has a word for these periodic attacks on Jews – *bunt*; some eighty people were killed before the 1892 attack petered out.

Interior of the Hughes' mansion, with potted palm. Courtesy of Glamorgan Record Office

The New Russia Company Pavilion at the Nizhnyi Novgorod Exposition 1896. Courtesy of: National Library of Finland

Yet the prosperity of Hughesovka continued throughout the 1890s. Although Ivor Hughes cut down on the fines imposed during his father's regime, the Hughes sons largely stuck to both the products and the policies of Hughes Senior. In 1895 and again in 1900, shareholders in the New Russia Company were delighted to learn that each original share had quadrupled, and in 1896 the Company put on an elaborate display of its wares at the Nizhnyi Novgorod Exposition of Arts and Industries. Set within a neoclassical temple display was a wrought iron potted palm; it seems that New Russia employee Alexey Mertsalov had been invited up to the Hughes mansion to see the original living plant that the family kept in its sitting room before making his remarkable replica.

The Welsh continued to enjoy their position at the top end of the town's hierarchy and Leeza Wiskin recalled how, on at least one occasion, "we rode out gaily in huge haycarts, our picnic lunch following, not in a small basket but in another haycart, complete with samovar for making tea."[33] The brothers and sisters of the James family, originally from Maesteg, brought up a total of thirty children in Hughesovka, all of them born there.

Arthur Hughes, the third eldest son of the founder, got married in Swansea but soon returned to Hughesovka where his children grew up. When they were old enough, he brought over a Welsh tutor for them: Annie Gwen Jones. At first she found the transition difficult: "I shall never forget the feeling

of utter loneliness which seized me as we journeyed over the bare, treeless, unending plains of the steppes – little wonder that *hiraeth* (longing) for my homeland almost overpowered me. But the varied interests of the strange life around me and the natural desire and curiosity to see everything helped me to feel at home in Hughesovka."[34]

An important means of helping her feel at home were the musical soirées held at Arthur Hughes's house: "Once a week we were privileged to hear music of the highest quality." A programme from the 1890s records that the repertoire included not only "Turkey Rhubarb" and "Bye-bye baby, bye-bye" but also, sung to a plaintive melody, "Adieu to dear Cambria" –

Adieu the dear land of the forests and fountains
The fate that divides us I deeply deplore,
Thy vales, fertile fields and thy wild heaving
                         mountains,
Alas I may dwell in that beauty no more.

Annie Jones seemed to have found some comfort in the beauty of a Ukrainian winter and recalled: "Our drives on sledges across the glittering snow with the troika bells ringing musically in the clear air. There was a touch of adventure in sledge drives over the steppes, for frequently wild dogs, half wolves, would follow us and our driver Ivan had to use his whip to keep them at a safe distance from us."[35]

The Hughes family had imported a pack of

hounds and clearly enjoyed the opportunities for hunting, sailing, golfing and fancy dress balls which were often shared with better-off Russians. But Annie Jones was conscious of the vulnerability of the privileged world in which she lived: "We lived in a large one-storeyed house in the midst of a large garden surrounded by high walls for the sake of security and we had night watchmen guarding the place."[36]

There were sharp class divides in Wales at that time but not as acute as those she saw in Hughesovka: "What strikes me immensely is the wide enormous unbridged gulf between the upper and lower classes of Russia. Unfortunately there are only two real classes. There is no real middle class; the chief mainstay and backbone of a country. The well born Russian despises and spurns the low born mouzek or peasant and treats him on most occasions more like a dog than a human being."[37]

Although the Welsh and the Russians met socially, there were tensions even amongst the better off on both sides. In 1896 the Congress of Mining Industrialists of South Russia pointed out that of the 267 technicians in the Donbass, 137 were "foreigners", i.e. not Russian nor Ukrainian, and demanded that they should be required to pass an exam in Russian. At the bottom of the Hughesovka hierarchy were the miners, often moving out of the pits back to the fields at harvest time and so seen by employers as "a wave of all sorts of working people, who seeing themselves as newcomers, are an element little-disciplined and easily drawn into all sorts of disorders."[38]

Perhaps these rumblings suggest why the Hughes brothers tried to sell the New Russia Company in 1898 (although they weren't offered what they regarded as an acceptable price). However reluctant they were to stay, they still resisted cautious attempts to make Hughesovka less of a company town – even sanitation and health care was run by them. As Professor Friedgut puts it, "the dogged insistence of the New Russia Company on maintaining its total control of the settlement's life prevented the development of grassroot institutions that might have created pressure for broader participatory institutions."[39]

Trade unions were illegal in Russia so discontent tended to find expression in a violent form. The governor of nearby Ekaterinoslav, F. E. Keller, wrote in 1902 that "In general the mine workers are less dangerous than the factory workers in terms of their propensity for disorder and receptivity to different types of propaganda." But after St. Petersburg's 'Bloody Sunday' in 1905, when troops fired on peaceful demonstrators, killing some 200 of them, injuring 800,[40] and setting off a wave of strikes and demonstrations throughout Russia, it was the miners who initiated a strike in Hughesovka. The town's Soviet of Workers Deputies excitedly declared that "Workers and other salaried persons bearing on their shoulders the struggle for liberation, have plunged into the final struggle for freedom."[41]

The political demands emanating from St. Petersburg and reflected throughout Russia were, says Orlando Figes, "remarkably uniform – the convocation of a constituent assembly elected by universal suffrage."[42] But a march to the Hughesovka factory by pro-democracy demonstrators, many of them Jewish, ended brutally, with the factory workers rallying to the defence of their workplace and throwing some of the leaders of the demonstration alive into the blast furnaces.

This was the year in which the Hughes brothers decided that, even if they couldn't get the price they were after, it was time to leave Hughesovka; only Arthur Hughes maintained a home address there. But by then, apart from the still strong Welsh contingent in the town, there was another strong Hughes connection. While Gwyn and I were in Donetsk, we made a discovery that provided a quite different perspective on the family of stern capitalists. It seems that John James Hughes, the founder's son, had a Russian mistress, Praskovia Sergeevna Polovinkina, his housekeeper. We were introduced to Nina Ivanovna Bulgakova, a rather genteel Russian lady in her eighties, who told us that John Hughes Junior had said to Praskovia, her grandmother, that he loved her very much but that it was impossible for them to marry because he already had a wife back in Britain. He did, however, make sure that Praskovia lived comfortably and there were regular presents to the child of their relationship, Ivan Metelenko.

Nina Ivanovna told us that, despite Ivan's

Praskovia Sergeevna Polovinkina, John James Hughes's mistress, and Ivan Metelenko, the child of their relationship.
Courtesy of: Sergei Kharitonov

31

striking resemblance to John Hughes Senior, she had kept quiet about the Hughes connection during most of her life because it would have been dangerous to admit descent from a capitalist during the Stalin years. We sat alongside her samovar politely drinking tea and chatting about Hughes's "unofficial wife", as the Donetsk descendants now call her, and I remember Gwyn longing for the tea party - even more prolonged because we were lighting and filming it - to end. For him, filming in the local pit had been bad enough but two hours of trying to make small talk to Nina Ivanovna in his few words of Russian was becoming more than he could stand. As the cameraman asked for yet another take, he muttered to me, "I'd sooner be back in that damn pit."

Most of the Hughes family, including John Hughes Junior, moved to St. Petersburg around 1905 and increasingly the day-to-day running of Hughesovka passed to local managers. The aftermath of Bloody Sunday led to the Czar's decision to permit the election of a Duma, an indirectly-elected assembly with a consultative role, and there now seemed to be the possibility of democratic change in Russia.

By the time the Hugheses left, their town had grown to 50,000, nearly a fifth of whom were employed by the New Russian Company - 5000 factory workers and 4500 coal miners. Despite labour disaffection, the factory was soon working at full capacity again and electricity began to replace steam power. Medhurst, the local British consul, was reassuring. "I ran down to Hughesovka to ascertain the real state of things," he wrote to Sir Edward Grey at the Foreign Office on 23 February 1906. "I returned convinced that there appeared to be no cause for apprehension… The strike leaders and most of the suspects are either in prison or have disappeared and the men generally appear only anxious to earn their wages in peace."[43]

Nevertheless the Foreign Office advised Evan Evans, at home on leave in 1906, not to return because of the unrest there and William Chambers, the assistant chief engineer at the New Russia Company, was shot at and slightly injured. The few members of the Social Democratic Party of Russia, a revolutionary party despite its name, tried to channel the unrest towards a demand for fundamental change but the line taken by their pamphlets suggests that they were whistling in the dark: "Acquaint yourselves with the law and prepare to be firm and unwavering defenders of the working proletariat… Enough sleeping comrades!"[44] Tiny though the Social Democratic Party was, it had sharp internal divisions – much of the energy of its members went into the complex ideological arguments between the Menshevik or Minority faction and those, led by Lenin, who claimed to be the Bolsheviks or the Majority.

Both factions would have been aware of the high accident rates at Hughesovka's mines and steel works. In 1903 eight New Russia employees were injured every day and the flying slag of the forging and rolling mills was a special hazard – nearly half of the steel works's labour force was injured each year.[45] But the state authorities as well as the employers were on the look out for any signs of dissent: coal owner Advakov wrote that "So much material had been gathered by them" (he was referring to the police and the Ministry of the Interior) "regarding the history of the Hughes factory that they know the situation in the mines quite as well as we do."[46]

Communications between the revolutionaries seems to acknowledge the extent of the control over the Hughesovka workers. Veniamin Ermoshenko, a Bolshevik miner who used the pen name of 'Young Miner', wrote in 1913 of "Silence. Not a sound of public activity is to be heard from the giant factory of 12,000 workers."[47] The place was surrounded by spies and repression, blundering in the darkness, he claimed.

But events elsewhere in Europe soon brought about a dramatic change. In August 1914 Elizabeth Perry wrote to her sister Margaret, reassuring her that all the family was well but adding, "The war was started so suddenly no one knew anything about it. Isn't it an awful thing to happen, one can hardly believe it."[48] Many of the British workers in Hughesovka immediately volunteered to join the British army and the touching photograph overleaf was taken of them on the station platform in Hughesovka just before they left, one of them, an engineer named Willie Clark, proudly holding a Union Jack. His Russian wife ruefully recalled later that he only told her he was signing up for the army after he had already done so.

Most of Russian public opinion, like that in Wales, seems to have supported the war against Germany at its outset. But, to his delight, Gwyn came across the work of a Ukrainian writer with revolutionary sympathies who turned up in Hughesovka soon after the war started and saw another side of the town. Too short sighted for military service, Konstantin Paustovsky got a job working in ordnance factories and was eventually moved to the Hughes's factory, booming because of the work generated by the war, including the manufacture of armaments.

Gwyn and I managed to locate the very hotel he stayed at and Gwyn strode up its stairs delivering the piece to camera he had written, in a state of high excitement: "He stayed here at what was once the Great Britain hotel (photo overleaf). Today it's rather charming but when Paustovsky stayed here the place stank of stale cabbage, medicine – and face powder. All the bedsprings were broken, the maids received in their rooms day and night and every evening someone got their head bashed in with a snooker cue. From this cosy cot, Paustovsky went off to his job in the steel works."

In the *Slow Approach of Thunder* volume of his autobiography that covers his time in Hughesovka, Paustovsky gives a vivid description of the town – smoke "poured from the chimneys of the various workshops. It was yellow and stank like burned milk.

Willie Clark, holding the Union Jack, and other volunteers for the British Army leaving Hughesovka in 1914.
Courtesy of: Glamorgan Record Office

A startling crimson flame danced above the blast furnaces. Greasy soot dripped from the sky. Nothing in Hughesovka was white. Whatever had started out as white was blotchy, yellowish grey – shirts, sheets, pillowcases, curtains, dogs, horses, cats."[49]

His first experience of the Bessemer shop "was a terrifying sight. The molten iron ran in trenches in the ground, belching clouds of blood-red steam. Everything was either scarlet or coal black. The workers, lit by the glow of the molten metal, looked like demons from hell… Everything around you roared, screeched, clanked, jangled, thudded, smoked and hissed with steam. Through all the din you heard a long drawn out ''ware!'ware!' – a worker with a red hot barrow hurried past (and if you didn't jump your clothes began to smoulder) while overhead, a crane swung, balancing an equally hot pig in its claws."[50]

Gwyn was attracted to Paustovsky not only by his lively writing style but also – naturally – by his politics. Like Gwyn from a middle-class background, he didn't identify himself with either the Bolsheviks or the Mensheviks but there was no doubt about which side he would be on if revolution erupted in Russia. While he was carrying out his job of examining shell cases at the Hughes factory, he found a duplicated leaflet had been slipped into one of the cases. On top were the words "Workers of the World Unite" and, when he read it, he discovered that it was a Bolshevik proclamation calling on the soldiers to stop fighting an imperialist war and turn their guns against the enemy at home. He put the leaflet back in the shell case and when he returned from his lunch it was gone. His fellow workers looked at him and smiled – but no one said a word.

Paustovsky wasn't the only one who realised that something was afoot in Hughesovka. In 1916 the Hughes brothers sold the New Russia Company to a Russian/French consortium. A year later Hughesovka was in the throes of revolution.

The Great Britain hotel, Hughesovka. Courtesy of: Andrew Butko

CHAPTER FOUR – REVOLUTION

On 6 May 1915, a statue to Czar Alexander II was unveiled in Hughesovka, to mark the 50th anniversary of his decree ending serfdom. He had been assassinated soon after that decree but local peasants wanted to express their gratitude for their liberation by contributing 6650 roubles to the cost of the statue. The band of the local technical college played in celebration and a Russian journalist, visiting from Petrograd more than a year later, could still write optimistically, "I see the hammer of labour beating, strongly and soberly, assuring our lives and our radiant future."[51]

But the workers of the New Russia Company saw things rather differently. Many of them had been deferred from military service in the war against Germany because of their work in an arms-related industry and so did not experience directly the growing resentment about conscription. But the word was out about heavy military defeats on the Northwestern Front, and the administrative incompetence that had led to it, was now beginning to seep through. At Tannenberg, the German army killed or wounded 70,000 Russians and had taken 100,000 prisoner; Samsonov, the Russian general responsible for the debacle, shot himself.

A report from the Director of the Russian Police to the Ministry of Interior spelt out the problems – "the irregularity of the food supply and the rising cost of living are explained as either lack of ability or lack of will of the central government to deal with these problems and for this reason the attitude towards (the government) is extremely negative… Everywhere and in all sections of the population, there is war-weariness and hunger for the most rapid peace, no matter on what terms it may be concluded."[52]

Hughesovka was soon directly affected by the crisis. In February 1917 the chief engineer of its mines reported, "All the enterprises report a general shortage of flour, barley, oil and other food products."[53] The refusal of soldiers in St. Petersburg, now renamed as Petrograd, to use their guns against demonstrators, which had triggered the first stage of the revolution there, was replicated in Hughesovka – soldiers called to intervene against a miners strike refused to move, expressing sympathy for the miners.

On March 2nd Czar Nicholas II abdicated and the next day 2000 workers from the New Russia factory met to hear reports on the war and the revolution, and to elect delegates to a local soviet. No sooner had it been elected than it declared that "power in the settlement of Hughesovka had been transferred to the Soviet of Workers Deputies" and set about disarming the police. Soviets, ad hoc councils of workers, were springing up in industrial areas all over Russia and rapidly became an alternative source of power.

A British/Russian tea party in Krivoi Rog near Hughesovka in 1915. Courtesy of: Glamorgan Record Office

One of those elected to the Hughesovka Soviet was Nikita Khrushchev, representing the nearby Rutchenka mine where he worked as a mechanic, though he later claimed to have played for the New Russia football team. Khrushchev became a Bolshevik, the self-proclaimed Majority faction of the Social Democratic Party, and Soviet Union historians have suggested that Hughesovka was by now a Bolshevik stronghold. But Professor Friedgut reckons that they only had nine members during the war years and says that "the Bolsheviks of the Donbass began their existence as a small, uninfluential and unpopular group." During the May Day demonstration in 1917, the Bolsheviks were attacked and 2000 Donbass miners gave their support to the Mensheviks, declaring that the Bolsheviks were "leading Russia to ruin with their agitation."[54]

The British Embassy in Petrograd sent a Mr Dickinson to Hughesovka to report on the situation and in September 1917 he filed a remarkably sympathetic report to the Foreign Office: "The workmen have been rottenly treated in the past, paid starvation wages and kept down in every possible way, while the mills made huge profits; now they are getting their own back and the wonder is to me that they have not gone further than they have."[55]

Many history books conflate what happened throughout Russia in 1917 to 'the Russian revolution'. In fact there were two, the second more like a coup d'état than a revolution. During 1917 the provisional government, whilst continuing to fight against Germany and its allies, had organised an election to an assembly that would determine the new constitution of the now Czarless nation.

But the Bolsheviks won just 10 million votes, twenty-four per cent of the total, and responded by closing down the Constituent Assembly by force. They had been advocating "All power to the Soviets" but had abandoned that approach when it became clear that the Bolsheviks could not control them. "It was revealing of Lenin's attitude towards the Soviets", writes historian Orlando Figes, "in whose name his regime was to be founded, that whenever they failed to serve the interests of his party, he was ready to ditch them."[56]

Hughesovka was in a revolutionary ferment, Khrushchev later recalling that "red flags were flying and huge meetings taking place."[57] By 1917 most Welsh workers had risen to foreman or managerial class at the New Russia Company and, far from being sympathetic to revolution, were more likely to become the target of angry workers. Frederick Loxley was 'wheelbarrowed' out of the factory and Leah Steel, wife of Thomas Steel, a works manager, gave a vivid description of the upheaval that swept though the town.

"In our area mobs of people roamed around claiming everything as their own, but they never took away or claimed anything from our home," she wrote. "At one time a mob came and demanded to see my husband, who came out and asked them what they wanted. They said, 'You have a lot of silver in the house, and it now belongs to us.' He replied, 'You people presented it to me as a gift on my 25th anniversary, if you want it back, take it." They murmured among themselves, then said, 'It is true, it is yours, please keep it.'"[58] Whether the people the Steels saw simply as 'a mob' were workers from the New Russia factory, they do not tell us.

Leah Steel recalled that "the Revolution was abhorrent to my husband and he decided that our family should leave Russia for good, as did other families."[59] Nina Ivanovna told Gwyn Williams and myself about the moment when many of the Welsh decided that their time was up: "I remember so well the British looking anxious, going in carriages to Karavanovo… I can still see their faces now." The mistress of John Hughes Junior was even more distressed: "My granny was very sorry for them and tears were running down her face."

In his youth, Gwyn had been inspired by the account of revolution in Russia recorded in films like *October,* and in books like John Reid's *Ten Days that Shook the World*. He and I had once walked reverentially around the battleship *Aurora*, whose gunfire attack on the Winter Palace in Petrograd began the second revolution of 1917. But it was becoming clear that workers in Hughesovka in 1917 interpreted the attack, not through the prism later supplied by pro-Bolshevik journalists and film makers, but as a ruthless bid to seize power. "The interpretation put on the events in Petrograd lent legitimacy to putting the Bolsheviks beyond the pale of the united democratic camp," writes Professor Friedgut. "In the Donbass, even more than in most of Russia, it appeared that the Bolsheviks were on their way from unpopularity to total ignominy."[60]

Gwyn was too good a historian to allow his own romantic view of the Bolsheviks to get in the way of the truth about what had happened in Hughesovka. When we were making our television series on the town, we climbed to the top of a local slagheap and he delivered a piece to camera describing what happened next: "In the autumn of 1917, public order broke down in one last god-awful outbreak of *bunt*. The local Soviet ordered the destruction of eight million litres of vodka which had accumulated during

the war. The town went mad."

It seems that soldiers of the local garrison then joined in an orgy of drinking, shops were looted and Jews fled. "When a workers militia marched up to restore order," said Gwyn, "they were denounced as defenders of the bourgeoisie and driven off. In the end local Soviets had to send in 1500 soldiers under the command of Bolshevik and Social Revolutionary commissars. It was only after they threatened to bombard the town with artillery that order was restored."

Khrushchev had now begun to play an important role in the town. It was here in 1917 that he had the good fortune to meet Lazar Moiseievich Kaganovitch, later to become Stalin's deputy and an important patron. According to historian Simon Sebag Montefiore, the local boss, despite his sympathies with Trotsky, made a favourable impression on the Bolshevik elite: "Resembling a cannonball more than a whirlwind, Khruschev's bright porcine eyes, chunky physique and toothy smile with its golden teeth, exuded primitive coarseness and Promethean energy but camouflaged his cunning."[61]

In St. Petersburg, Vladimir de Boursac, the great grandson of John Hughes Senior, and just three years old at the time, had a rather different kind of good luck: "I and my sister were taken away by our cook because the Bolsheviks were looking for us. I was put in a cupboard by this cook and told to be quiet because the Bolsheviks were going to come and

Poster anticipating the success of the Bolsheviks.
Courtesy of: Glamorgan Record Office

search the house for us. And I stayed in this cupboard and didn't make a sound at all… The Bolsheviks went in, searched the house and didn't find us."

Vladimir's father Serge, who had married Kyra Hughes, John Hughes's granddaughter, was caught by a Bolshevik patrol, apparently whilst out on a hunting expedition. Vladimir told Gwyn and I that "of course they recognised him as not one of them", and went on to calmly tell us about his own father's grim death. The Bolsheviks had forced him and his two companions to dig their own graves then buried them alive. Serge's widow had subsequently managed to escape from Russia, taking Vladimir and his sister with her to France.

On 4 January 1918 the New Russia Company was formally nationalised. A decree of the Praesidium of the All Russian Supreme Economic Council declared that, in view of the company's importance to the Soviet state and the inability of the owners to maintain the operation of its enterprises, it would henceforward be managed by the state. This does not indicate that Hughesovka had been won over to the Bolshevik's position; on the contrary "in mid March 1918, the Bolsheviks lost the town's confidence, and had it not been for the intervention of the Donbass military revolutionary committees," says Professor Friedgut, "they would have lost control of the [Hughesovka] Soviet."[62]

Although the Bolsheviks had ended the hated war, the Treaty of Brest-Litovsk seceded so much territory to Germany that many Russians saw it as a national humiliation. In Hughesovka, the Bolsheviks intensified their propaganda and poured in its activists but in the end, as in Petrograd, it was brute force that secured their control of the town. Though later denied by Soviet historians, it was military force, not workers' control, that gave Bolsheviks victory in Hughesovka six months after they had triumphed in Petrograd.

But this was not the end of the struggle – Russia, as well as most of Ukraine, now erupted into civil war and Hughesovka changed hands repeatedly. Helen Clark (married name Wareing), the daughter of a marriage between the aforementioned British engineer Willie Clark and a Russian woman he had met in the town, remembered it vividly: "Whichever was in control of the district, we always had to billet some of the officers. As far as I remember, they were all courteous, brought their own rations, and did not take anything away; it was not their fault that they were crawling with lice."[63]

In most of Russia, the war was between the Whites, fighting to restore the Czar, and the Reds. But in the south east of Ukraine there was a third force, the Anarchists, led by Nestor Makhno, a man who Orlando Figes describes as being of "legendary status among the local peasants", standing for "a stateless peasant revolution based on the local self-rule of the free and autonomous Soviets that had emerged in the countryside during 1917."[64]

Although he formed a brief alliance with the Bolsheviks against the White Russians, Makhno's libertarianism was anathema to the Reds – and Helen Clark wasn't much of a fan either: "The most notorious band was led by a crazy man called Makhno, and nothing was safe from them; they took everything they wanted and shot anyone who protested. On one of these 'visits' to our house, the bandits demanded food and when our servant told them we had none and asked them to go, one of them pushed her against the wall of the kitchen, pulled out his gun, called her all sorts of names for protecting her bourgeois employers, and threatened to shoot her if she did not produce some food. I was in the doorway paralysed with terror, watching my mother begging them to take everything they wanted but to leave the servant unharmed. Suddenly – for no reason I could see – they vanished as quickly as they had come."[65]

By 1921 not only the White Russians but also those on the left opposed to the Bolsheviks had been defeated. Trotsky had once described the Kronstadt sailors as the "pride and glory of the Russian revolution" but they were as much anarchists as Bolsheviks and in 1921 on the fourth anniversary of the 1917 revolution the sailors proclaimed that "workers and peasants need freedom. They do not want to live by the decrees of the Bolsheviks. They want to control their own destinies." Within a month, Trotsky and the Bolsheviks had crushed them, as brutally as he did Makhno's forces in Ukraine. Trotsky then proudly announced that "at last the Soviet government with an iron broom, has rid Russia of anarchism."[66]

Nestor Makhno's anarchist army. Courtesy of: Shevchenko Library and Archive

Even by 1922 the Bolsheviks in Hughesovka were still a small minority – of the 63,000 New Russian workers, only 70 were members. Nikita Khrushchev, an early member, became a key figure once the Red Army had re-conquered the town. Few there could have been surprised when it now had its name changed, the Bolsheviks declaring that it was "unthinkable that the proletarian centre of the Donbass should bear the name of the exploiter Hughes."[67]

The first name chosen was Trotsky but it wasn't long before he was out of favour and in June 1924 the name of Stalino was chosen instead. It was named after the Russian word for steel, not after Josef Vissarionoich Djugashvili who had given himself the alias of Stalin, by implication 'man of steel', when the Bolsheviks were still an underground organisation. Vladimir Lenin, the leader of the Bolsheviks, had once seen Stalin as the "wonderful Georgian";[68] it wasn't long before Lenin and the newly-labelled town of Stalino began to change their opinion of him.

"Insurgent Ukraine" cartoon. Best endeavours were made to secure copyright

CHAPTER FIVE – THE SHADOW OF STALIN

If the dream of the oppressed workers of Hughesovka was to turn it into a city run by and for the workers, they were soon disappointed. Once the Bolsheviks had won back control, not only in Stalino but throughout the whole of what became the Soviet Union, they started to crush their former comrades, arresting some 5000 Mensheviks in 1921 and subjecting the Socialist Revolutionaries to a show trial. The Independent Labour Party, strong in Wales, kicked up about it but from most of the Welsh left, there was a deafening silence.

"The suppression of the Kronstadt rebellion had a shattering effect on socialists throughout the world,"[69] writes Orlando Figes. Trotsky's suppression of the sailors who were once the vanguard of the Russian revolution, may have shattered some socialists but not all. S. O. Davies represented the Dowlais district of the Red International of Labour Unions on a visit to Moscow and later toured the Don mining valleys. When he returned he wrote in the Colliery Workers Magazine of "that truly wonderful miracle – Russia in December 1922!" He wrote of "the supreme pleasure that is felt by these emancipated people as they jealously and proudly watch the growth of a new culture" and believed he was seeing "how the most brutal autocracy can be transformed into a commonwealth where useful work and indispensable service lead not to penury and repression, but to freedom and the exaltation of man in his dominion over material things."[70]

Meanwhile Helen Clark and her family were struggling to survive in Rutchenko, a village near Stalino. "Sometimes I went with my aunt Sonia to collect our bread ration and I remember seeing people sitting or lying at the roadside with their hands stretched towards us, begging for bread; they were grey-faced and emaciated and could hardly move."

After Helen's father Willie had gone off to fight in the British army during the First World War, he had found it difficult to return, so she was living with her mother and grandparents: "We never had enough food, but we were luckier than town-dwellers; we had a large garden with fruit trees where we could grow vegetables and grandmother kept a cow and some chickens, but we did not see sugar, tea, flour or meat for weeks. My grandmother made and remade our clothes, concocted coffee out of roasted acorns and tea out of dried-up grated carrots, looked after the poultry and also managed to find something to give the numerous beggars who came to the door."[71]

Though still a child, Helen soon became aware of the new ideology: "One day, when I was coming home from school one of the bigger boys in the class, obviously repeating something he had heard from an adult, said, 'Your grandfather is a bourgeois.' This was the most insulting word anyone could use, and I hit him. He was so furious that he knocked me into the snow and would have beaten me black and blue if a peasant woman who was passing had not intervened."

I remember going to see Helen at her home in Aberystwyth not long before she died. She was charming and helpful, still with a distinct Russian accent and remarkably good humoured about the Bolshevik regime, despite the fact that in the 1920s it began removing books from her grandfather's home to a new library and theatre, part of a campaign to liquidate literacy: "Fortunately for us they did not then approve of foreign authors, and by the time they reached our house with their cart they had already collected some books by Russian classical writers, so they took away only about half of Grandfather's books."[72]

Her grandfather was soon to lose his house as well as half his books. The village council decided it should become a club for local workers and the family's furniture was taken out of the house and dumped in the yard: "We were lucky – we lost a bit of furniture but we found a room eventually in another large house. But later on, when we knew that Khrushchev was in charge of the village Soviet, we always suspected that it may have been by his orders that we were moved out. But I've forgiven him – I always liked Mr Krushchev!"[73]

Many Russians and Ukrainians idealised the period after the Civil War had ended in 1921.

Gwyn and I talked to an old school teacher, Yulian Veldorovitch Schmilo, who we met while filming in his home town, and he told us, "I was very enthusiastic when I came here. I understood there was a lot of things to do and I had been sent here to help to reconstruct the Donbass region." Gradually the coal mines and steel works started functioning again – coal, steel and railway tracks were to be essential in the rebuilding of the state - and the town had piped water laid on for the first time. Literacy greatly improved throughout the Soviet Union, from thirty-five per cent of the population in 1907 to fifty-one per cent by 1926.

Even before Lenin's death in 1924, there had been both an easing of the party line about small scale capitalism with the introduction of the New Economic Policy and the beginning of 'korenitzatisiya', designed to broaden Communism's appeal to speakers of the Ukrainian language. The latter helped to teach thousands of peasants in the countryside around Stalino to read and write and there was an improvement in prospects for Stalino's manual workers too. The claim of OGPU, the regime's secret police, that they had discovered a "counter-revolutionary plot" in the Shakty coal mines of the Donbass by "bourgeois" engineers in 1928 led eventually to the arrest of half of all engineers and technical workers in the area, and the consequent swift promotion for those below them in the hierarchy. Historian Hiroaki Kuromiya argues that, throughout the Soviet Union, ambitious and politically reliable young workers were selected

Josef Stalin, made General Secretary of the Soviet Communist Party in 1922.

for promotion and that "the years 1928-31 were a period of enormous upward mobility for the working class."[74]

The NEP policy was now abandoned and Stalin, who by 1928 was indisputed leader of the Soviet Union, drove forward a policy of rapid industrialisation. This began with the first of a series of five-year plans and the song I remember older left wing friends singing, to the tune of "Green Grow the Rushes Oh!", recalls the rather naïve idealism that inspired Communists throughout the world at that time. The song concluded:

> Five for the years of the five year plan
> And four for the four years taken,
> Three, three the rights of man-o
> Two, two the worker's hands
> Working for his living-o
> One is workers unity
> And ever more shall be so.

Admiration for the Soviet Union wasn't confined to dedicated Communists; south Wales miners remembered with huge gratitude the support given to them by Russian trade unions during the 1926 lockout; Nine Mile Point pit, in the Sirhowy Valley, Monmouthshire, always referred subsequently to the grants that were dispensed to members at the time as 'Russian money.'[75]

But Welsh sympathisers in the 1920s knew little of what was going on inside the Soviet Union.

Rapid industrialisation there soon created an acute shortage of labour and OGPU, the regime's secret police, began drawing up a further list of those they designated as 'counter-revolutionaries' who were to be dealt "a crushing blow when the time comes,"[76] perhaps as a source of the slave labour Stalin knew he would require to implement his ambitious plans. The workers' newspaper *The Dictatorship of Labour* made the threat clear: "In the republic of labour, there is no room for parasites and idlers. They will either be shot or pulverised between the great millstones of labour."

When those millstones started to grind, the party demolished the cathedral in Stalino but most of the workers in the town were spared; it was the peasants in the villages around it that became the target of the party's rage about what it saw as the lack of revolutionary progress. "Militant Bolsheviks were increasingly afraid that the revolution would degenerate," writes Orlando Figes, "that it would sink in the 'kulak' mud, unless a new civil war was launched to subjugate the village to the town."[77] This, he argues, was the root of Stalin's civil war against the village, the civil war of collectivisation.

The Bolsheviks settled on a prime target, the better-off peasants or kulaks, deciding that it was they who were preventing sufficient food coming into the towns. Millions of peasants were forced to give up their smallholdings and join collective farms; in 1928, requisitioning brigades arrived in the villages of Ukraine demanding the surrender of a quantity of grain and meat.

"We will keep the Kulaks out of the collective farms" – Soviet poster. Courtesy of: Dr Margaret Siriol Colley

Those who resisted were labelled kulaks and in December 1929 Stalin announced the "liquidation of the kulaks as a class". Some were arrested, many shot and mass deportation began. Between 1930 and 1933 over two million peasants were sent into exile in

Gareth Jones, one of the very few journalists who revealed what was happening during the Ukraine famine.
Courtesy of: Dr Margaret Siriol Colley

Siberia and other underpopulated regions of Russia, and a further hundred thousand were sent to the prison camps of the Gulag.

Ukraine had been seen as the Soviet Union's grain store but the consequence of the deportations was that food output almost came to a standstill. Anyone spotted picking corn or hiding food, even to feed children, could be shot on the spot and the countryside around Stalino became the scene of starvation and famine.

But there was no mention of the disaster in local papers or even in the reports of most foreign correspondents based in the Soviet Union. One of the very few exceptions was a Welsh freelance journalist named Gareth Jones, born in Barry and the son of Annie Gwen Jones who, from 1889 to 1892, had been the tutor to the children of Arthur Hughes in Hughesovka. In the summer of 1930 Gareth Jones toured the Soviet Union and made a special effort to get to Stalino – or Hughesovka as he insisted on calling it. He made it on 17 August by taking a train there and, when he was able to write an uncensored letter outside Russia ten days later, told his parents what he had seen. "In the Donetsk Basin conditions are unbearable. Thousands are leaving. I shall never forget the night I spent in a railway station on the way to Hughesovka. One reason why I left Hughesovka so quickly was that all I could get to eat was a roll of bread – and that is all I had up to seven o'clock. Many Russians are too weak to work."[78]

This letter then became the basis for a report he had published in the *Western Mail* on 24 September 1930, under the headlines "Starving Miners Flight from Communism. Famous Steel Centre No Longer Prosperous". In it he wrote, "I obtained my ticket to Hughesovka, the Dowlais of Russia, the town founded and named after the Welshman John Hughes… Prosperity has abandoned Hughesovka for the time being. There is nothing in the shops… I decided to follow the example of the miners and to leave the Donetsk Basin for a place where I hoped to get something to eat. Such was my experience of the Glamorgan of Russia."

He returned to the Soviet Union in 1931 and again in 1933, providing a devastating report on conditions in Ukraine. "The Russian situation is absolutely terrible, famine almost everywhere, and millions dying of starvation. I tramped for several days through villages in the [sic] Ukraine, and there was no bread, many children had swollen stomachs, nearly all the horses and cows had died and the people themselves were dying… The peasants were eating the cattle fodder and had only a month's supply left. They told me that many had died of hunger… 'We are waiting for death' was my welcome."[79]

The reason for what became known as The Great Hunger is a matter of intense historical controversy even today. Insofar as the Soviet authorities acknowledged that any explanation was required at all, the imposition of collectivisation on Ukrainian peasants was justified as a necessary step towards modernising the rural economy. But deporting successful farmers and starving the rest could not possibly have increased the agricultural yield and many are drawn to the conclusion that this was, in the words of Anna Reid, "a deliberate genocidal attack on rural Ukraine."[80] This was after all the area – Ukraine – and the class – successful peasants – most resistant to the Bolsheviks. There was famine elsewhere in the Soviet Union but the higher grain quotas imposed on Ukraine – in 1932 Stalin increased Ukraine's grain procurement quota by forty-four per cent – ensured that death rates were substantially higher in the territory for which Stalin always seemed to have had a peculiar venom.

Historian Andrew Wilson acknowledges that The Great Hunger was deliberate and brutal but sees it as "part of an ideological rather than a national war. It pitted town against countryside… proletarian against peasant, poor peasant against 'rich' peasant, as much as Russian against Ukrainian."[81]

But most of the correspondents in the Soviet Union at the time denied that there was a famine at all, deliberate or accidental. A meeting of the Moscow press corps and Konstantin Umansky, the chief censor, decided to rubbish Gareth Jones's reports and at least one of those present, Eugene Lyons, had the grace to later admit to his unease about what followed. "We admitted enough to soothe our consciences, but in roundabout phrases that damned Jones as a liar. That filthy business disposed of, someone ordered vodka and 'zakuski',

Umansky joined the celebration, and the party did not break up until the early hours."[82]

Walter Duranty of the *New York Times* then wrote that "there is no famine or actual starvation, nor is there likely to be"[83] and Gareth Jones responded that censorship had turned Russian-based journalists into "masters of euphemism and understatements. Hence," he said, "they give 'famine' the polite name of 'food shortage' and 'starving to death' is softened down to read as 'widespread mortality from diseases due to malnutrition.'"

The Soviet authorities would have been only too glad to have seen Gareth Jones disposed of. But, ironically, it was while he was setting out to expose the duplicity of the Communists' arch enemies – the Japanese Fascists – that he met his end. Whilst digging out information about Japanese troop movements in Mongolia he was captured by Chinese bandits and, on 12 August 1935, shot three times. Some have seen the long hand of the Soviet secret police holding the gun that killed him[84] but a Japanese plot seems more likely.

The material conditions for those living in Stalino marginally improved in the early 30s, with its citizens getting piped water and a sewage system for the first time. But they could hardly be unaware of what was going on in the countryside around them. Yulian Schmilo told Gwyn and I that he lived near the cemetery in the town and that every evening he "saw carriages with corpses piled on them, they were taken somewhere to be dumped. Nobody knew these people, they were strangers here." The pain in his face was transparent as he recalled those terrible times. "They were forgotten. So many died. There were even cases of cannibalism. People were being starved to death."

Gwyn found these conversations deeply disturbing. He already knew about some of what we were being told but he had grown up in the 30s Depression when, as he put it, "Russia was a far-off place of strange photographs of even stranger leaders. Though, naturally, the Hope of the World!" Born in Dowlais in 1925 of schoolteacher parents, he grew up in an intensely political environment. "We burned and bled with our comrades in Spain… It was the idea of an International which gripped all of us by the throat."[85] So fired had he been that he went to the International Brigade office in Dowlais to volunteer to fight in Spain. A face had appeared over the high counter, looked down on the diminutive Gwyn and told him, "Son, come back when we're desperate."[86]

Yulian Schmilo had come to Stalino with the same sort of idealism. But, he told a glum Gwyn, "the Stalin period was like living under the sword of Damocles. I lived in this town and almost every day a black car would patrol the streets. It was called the Black Raven. We followed the car. It went to certain streets and took someone. The end. The man was no more."

He was describing the Great Terror of 1937-38, which hit towns like Stalino as brutally as the Great Hunger had hit the surrounding areas of countryside.

One of Yulian's friends, "a model Leninist", was taken away on his son's birthday for, he was told, five minutes. It wasn't until 19 years later that he came back home.

He was comparatively lucky. Simon Sebag Montefiore estimates that, during the Terror, some one and a half million were arrested and 700,000 shot.[87] Robert Conquest puts the figures even higher – asserting that two million died in the labour camps and that one million were executed.[88] As Anne Applebaum sees it, "1937 does mark a genuine watershed. For it was in this year that the Soviet camps temporarily transformed themselves from indifferently managed prisons in which people died by accident, into genuinely deadly camps where prisoners were deliberately worked to death, or actually murdered, in far larger numbers than they had been in the past."[89]

I remember Gwyn in Donetsk, forty years after these terrible events, wrestling with the form of words that he would use on camera when summing up both the Terror and his own feelings about it. He didn't hold back from describing the horrors of both famine and purges and then, with the ubiquitous statue of Lenin framed in the background, he said, "And as Stalino grew at breakneck pace, back in John Hughes's homeland, south Wales was devastated by the Depression. Thousands of people there looked to the Soviet Union as a beacon of hope, as I did myself. We knew little or nothing of the repression. We knew of the sacrifices – we saw them as the price paid by a heroic people building a new social order."

It was that heroic image that the Soviet propaganda machine aimed to project abroad during the 30s, hoping to divert attention from Stalin's show trials and rumours about the scale of the purges. The Donbass miner Alexey Stakhanov, who it was claimed had exceeded his coal-gathering quota by fourteen times, was cited as an exemplar of the heroic people. Representatives of the South Wales Miners Federation like Arthur Horner and Dai Lloyd Davies went to the Soviet Union as if on visits to the Holy Land. The latter brought back a relic, a banner from the working women of Krasnaya Presna Moscow, to 'Little Moscow' Maerdy and it now rests in the South Wales Miners Library in Swansea. The poet and Congregationalist Minister T. E. Nicholas, Niclas y Glais, visiting Russia in 1935, wrote ecstatically that:

> *Eithr gwelais wedd y ddaear yn cyfnewid*
> *A breuddwyd gwlad yn troi yn newydd wyrth,*
> *A chnawd a giau'n gwisgo'r hen addewid,*
> *A gwerin orfoleddus wrth y pyrth…*

What I did see was the earth in transformation
A country's dream becoming miraculously true.
I saw the old promise taking on flesh and blood,
And the common people joyful at the gates...[90]

Even the most devout of the Welsh admirers of the Soviet Union found it difficult to swallow the next twist of Stalin's policy. Unable to set up an anti-Nazi

Alexey Stakhanov, Donbass miner and Hero of Socialist Labour.
Courtesy of: Library of Congress

alliance with a wary Britain and France, the Soviet Union announced on 23 August 1939 what Gwyn called "the numbing horror of the Nazi-Soviet Pact", a non-aggression deal with Germany, its secret terms carving up eastern Europe between the two powers. Khrushchev, who had been an enthusiastic implementer of the Ukraine purges, was now moved to Poland where he "ruthlessly suppressed any sections of the population who might oppose Soviet power: priests, officers, noblemen, intellectuals were kidnapped, murdered and deported to eliminate the very existence of Poland."[91] By November 1940, one tenth of Poland's population had been deported, thirty per cent of whom were to die soon afterwards.

Stalin thought he had bought himself time but was in for a shock. On 22 June 1941, Nazi Germany invaded the Soviet Union. "That morning," Gwyn wrote, "my father broke with precedent and came into my bedroom with a cup of tea. 'You'll be all right now,' he said, 'they've gone into Russia.'" Although Gwyn's revered Soviet Union was now in danger, it meant that the embarrassment of the Nazi-Soviet pact could now be forgotten about and that the left could once again unite against the common enemy. Surely now, with the entry into the war of the mighty Red Army, Fascism would be defeated.

He rushed down to his local chapel to meet his young Communist contemporaries who were "hopping about and hugging themselves. Whatever happened now, we knew we had won. And as people filed past into morning service, we sang the *Internationale. Sotto voce*, of course."[92]

By then Helen Clark, "encountering discrimination and distrust of foreigners" in Moscow, had managed to get out, though some of her fellow workers with her British employer had been arrested and two briefly imprisoned during the 1930s. In spite of all her problems in the Soviet Union, she could still write that "it took me years to get used to living in England and to the lack of warmth in personal relations there. It was only when I came to live in Wales that I felt this warmth again."[93]

CHAPTER SIX – JACKBOOTS IN STALINO

Many in Ukraine shared Gwyn's elation at the news of the German invasion, although their motivation differed. In the two years before the attack, it is estimated that Khrushchev, now the First Secretary of the Ukrainian Communist Party, helped to organise the deportation of between 800,000 and 1.6 million people, ten to twenty per cent of the entire population of western Ukraine.[94] Most were Poles who, according to Khrushchev, failed to realize "that their culture would actually be enriched by the annexation of their lands to the Soviet Union."[95] In Lviv there were massacres of prisoners in the NKVD gaols as the Germans advanced. As Anna Reid puts it, many Ukrainians "believed Nazi rule could not possibly be any worse than Stalinism."[96]

Stalino, which had always been more Russian than Ukrainian, had little sympathy with the viewpoint of Ukrainian nationalists and 100,000 miners were mobilised to defend the Donbas, the Soviet Ruhr. The terrifying speed of the German advance forced the Red Army to retreat to the town early in October 1941 but by the end of the month it had fallen. Ukraine, soon occupied in its entirety, would now discover that the brutality of the Gestapo could indeed exceed even that of the NKVD.

The wholesale murder of Jews began almost immediately, most notoriously at Babiy Yar where 33,771 men, women and children were machine gunned down and shovelled into a ravine. Members of the Organisation of Ukrainian Nationalists, many of whom had at first seen the Nazis as liberators, soon learnt that Ukrainians too were regarded as 'Untermenschen', an inferior species, and dozens of OUN activists were arrested and executed. Before long a partisan force, known as the Ukrainian Insurgent Army or UPA, was operating underground throughout Ukraine.

The Nazis changed the name of the town back to Hughesovka, set up a prison camp in the House of Culture there and began to deport civilians to work as slave-labourers in Germany. Between the spring of 1942 and the summer of 1944, Germany sent over two million Ukrainians to the Reich as Eastworkers or 'Ostarbeiter', living and working in appalling conditions. Ninety-two thousand were to die in Stalino's own concentration camp before they got there. Gwyn stood at the eternal flame that still burns in their memory at the place where the camp once stood and stressed that throughout the occupation "the Germans got not a single ton of coal or steel out of Stalino." We found a Nazi propaganda newsreel that purported to show the opposite, Gwyn pointing out the shot of a workman at a Stalino pithead "wielding his peculiarly flaccid hammer."

During the purges, the Red Army had been a particular target of Stalin, 40,000 officers having

Jewish women and children driven towards a death pit in Volhynia in 1941. Courtesy of: Yad Vashem

been arrested. But many of those imprisoned then, or during the panic at the beginning of the war, were now reinstated. General Meretskov had been brutally beaten with rubber rods but was now taken out of his cell, cleaned up and brought back into the Kremlin so that he could be moved into a senior Red Army post. "Hello, Comrade Meretskov," said Stalin, according to Montefiore's account, "How are you feeling?"[97]

While conditions in the Gulag worsened for most, some were sent to the front in prisoner battalions. Gwyn and I met one of them, Vladimir Karpov, who had once made a joke about Stalin but was now ordered by his commanding officer to go behind enemy lines at night and bring back 'tongues', German prisoners who would be made to disclose information. After a couple of vodkas, he and Gwyn got on like a house on fire and we learnt that, because he had brought back 79 'tongues', he had been forgiven and awarded the Order of Lenin, the Soviet equivalent of the V.C. After Vladimir had touchingly recalled fellow soldiers who had been killed, and after the camera and filming lights for our documentary had gone, I heard him say to fellow war veteran Gwyn, "Best time of our lives, wasn't it?" Gwyn chortled agreement.

Gwyn felt the suffering of the Soviet people intensely. In 1985, whilst filming *Lest Who Forgets?* for BBC Wales, I saw him walking through the colossal cemetery in what was then Leningrad, deeply moved by how the music being played on loudspeakers included that of Mozart and Beethoven. He saw this as the cemetery's interpretation of the war as one against Fascism, not the German people. He had a vivid memory of being in the sixth form at Cyfarthfa Grammar School during a visit by a Russian trio, at a time when the BBC refused to play the *Internationale* as the Soviet anthem on the grounds that it was not a national anthem. He described with animation on camera what happened next in the Nevsky Prospekt, a crowd of Russians gathering behind him.

"After the concert, the leader said that he understood that there was some problem over the *Internationale* so they would sing a Russian folk song. Up stood Miss Davenport, the headmistress of the girls' school – English, tall, forbidding, Tory, a walking war memorial – 'I'm sure,' she said, fixing everybody with a gimlet eye, 'I'm sure that we would love to hear the *Internationale*.' And our gang was going mad at the back." Gwyn then started to sing:

> Then comrades come rally
> And the last fight let us face…

At this point the crowd in the Nevsky Prospect joined in, singing along in Russian:

> The Internationale
> Unites the human race.

In 1943 the heroism of the Red Army at the siege of

Gwyn Williams singing the *Internationale* in the Nevsky Prospekt, Leningrad in 1985. Courtesy of: Hazel Gower

Stalingrad did seem to unite the human race, at least that part of it that wasn't Fascist. Vasily Grossman was in a position to observe it at first hand as the reporter for the army newpaper *Red Star*. A Ukrainian Jew, born in the predominantly Jewish town of Berdichev, he had worked as a mine inspector and chemistry teacher in Stalino before becoming a writer. Despite his misgivings over Stalin's rule, he found a new sense of hope at the front line, which he expressed in *Life and Fate*, his monumental novel about the war: "Nearly everyone believed that good would triumph, that honest men, who hadn't hesitated to sacrifice their lives, would be able to build a good and just life."[98] During the siege of Stalingrad, he wrote in his diary of the Black Division, the Donbass miners division, standing firm against an attack by a hundred German tanks. "Miners don't retreat!" they shouted and Grossman quotes Colonel Zinoviev, their commander as saying, "They sleep in the forest when it's minus 35 degree. They aren't afraid of tanks. 'A mine is more frightening,' they say."[99]

In Wales there was a great surge of support for the Soviet Union in a moment of amnesia about the Nazi-Soviet pact and the Communist Party's opposition to the war effort from 1939 to 1941. Many on the left pressed for a second front in western Europe to take some of the pressure off the Red Army, Nye Bevan writing in *Tribune* that "everywhere where men gather one subject is fiercely debated – when are we going to back up in Europe the Homeric resistance of the Soviet Union?"[100]

Khrushchev, despite having been involved in the unsuccessful attempt to retake Kharkov which had so incurred Stalin's wrath, had become the political representative on the Military Council at Stalingrad and, according to Montefiore, subsequently inflated his role there.[101] He was later to claim a key part in planning the pincer movement that led to the surrender of the German general Paulus and his entire Sixth Army.

As the Nazis were pushed back, Khrushchev was promoted to Lieutenant-General and was involved in the battle of Kursk, the biggest tank battle ever fought. He could now resume his role as leader of the Communist Party in Ukraine and was ultimately responsible for the organisation of the partisans operating behind German lines. On 8 September 1943, the Red Army pushed forward into Stalino.

It wasn't to be until 1944 that the Welsh left got the second front it had been arguing for and, when it came in June, Gwyn Williams was part of it. He was in a signals unit that landed on Normandy and, on the very first occasion on which I filmed him, he described it to a crowd at a demonstration on the steps of Merthyr library in 1981, with the rain a deluge. I have been present at speeches by Nye Bevan, Michael Foot and Bernadette Devlin but this was the most thrilling piece of oratory I have ever witnessed.

After spending a terrified night in a foxhole he'd dug, he had woken with a sense of "vaulting exhilaration" as he looked back at the beach on which he had landed.

"Ukraine is Free!" Soviet poster 1944.
Courtesy of: Shevchenko Library and
Archive

"I saw a sight I'd never seen before and which no-one will ever see again. The sea was black with our ships, the sky was black with our planes, the beaches were black with our men and our machines, punching into Hitler's bloody Europe. And I felt that was our vengeance, after twenty years of defeat since 1926, that was our vengeance."

The Red Army advancing through Ukraine must have felt a similar excitement, intensified by the discovery of what the Nazis had been guilty of as occupiers, sometimes assisted by Ukrainian collaborators. When Grossman reached his home town of Berdychiv, he discovered that almost its entire population of 39,000 people had been fenced into a ghetto and then exterminated. His reports were censored because they revealed that Ukrainians had helped with the massacre, even though he also acknowledged that some had enabled a few Jews to escape. The reports did not mention that his own mother had been one of the fatalities; he was haunted by the fact that he had not helped her to get out of Ukraine before the Nazi occupation and wrote letters to her for years afterwards.

Gwyn had briefly come across survivors of the Nazis, on Victory in Europe Day in Paris, which he described to camera in the Teliesyn production *Lest Who Forgets?* on the fortieth anniversary in 1985, while walking through the Winter Palace Square in what was then Leningrad. On that day and since, veterans wear their medals and children give flowers to any veteran they happen to spot. "There weren't any British soldiers there so a friend of mine and I stole – well, borrowed, a Union Jack and started marching up the Champs Elysees. A great crowd formed around us, some of them sang Tipperary – 'It's a long vay to Teepperaree' and so on. They fell silent when a bus came through carrying back prisoners liberated from Hitler's concentration camps; they were still in their striped pyjamas…."

At this precise moment, with no prearrangement, a little Russian girl came up to Gwyn who was arrayed with his service medals and gave him – of all things – a daffodil. He said, "*Diolch*" and continued to camera, "All around them, we sang and shouted and drank champagne and waved flags. They just stared at us, they seemed completely bewildered. They were grey, they looked alien, they never smiled. Then suddenly there was a jeep with three Russian officers in it. The crowd took the Russians out of the jeep, lifted them on their shoulders and carried them up the Champs Elysees."

There was no such welcome for the Red Army in Ukraine. The '*Ostarbeiter*' returning from Germany were regarded with intense suspicion by the party faithful and, as the NKVD moved back into Ukraine, thousands of ordinary people who had found themselves on the wrong side of the line after the Nazi invasion, and many Red Army soldiers who had been taken captive by the Germans, were arrested and deported – even partisans who had fought behind the lines were sometimes sent straight off to the Gulag.

Gwyn, of course, knew nothing of this and his first encounter with the Red Army at Magdeburg

Gwyn Williams meeting a Russian naval veteran in Red Square in 1985. Courtesy of: Hazel Gower

ensured that he maintained the romantic image he had had of an army of liberators. "One of them briefly became a friend. His name was Vlado, he was from Kiev and he wanted to become a doctor. Vlado and I used to converse in pigeon German. One day we climbed a little hill and, like two boy scouts, mixed our blood and swore that never in our lives would we go to war together."

This was in 1945, just before the Cold War began.

CHAPTER SEVEN – A TOWN WITHOUT MEN

"Stalino had been devastated by the war, its pits flooded, its population decimated," said Gwyn in his film voiceover for *Hughesovka and the New Russia*. "So dreadful had been the losses that for many years there were twelve women for every man. It was women who worked the pits." Forty years later we found one of those women, Maria Osipenko, and Gwyn chatted to her on a wooden bench outside her home about life at the coalface. "We began to crawl – it was so hot, it was like an oven. You couldn't even turn round."

Over some touching archive film of demobilised Red Army soldiers returning to their families, Gwyn's commentary said, "The soldiers came home to a time of hope, a time of tears. I too came home after the war to a welcome and a time of hope. As a young Communist, I looked to this country for a major revival of that hope."

Those hopes were soon to be dashed – physically Stalino and the rest of Ukraine were gradually restored but the Communist Party was deeply suspicious about what had happened during the Nazi occupation. Montefiore alleges that Khrushchev, now the Ukraine's Premier as well as its Party Secretary, ordered the assassination of bishops of the Ukraine's distinctive Uniate church and the arrest of almost a million Ukrainians – "a colossal crime which approached the deportation of the kulaks in brutality and scale."[102] It is hardly surprising then that the Ukrainian Insurgent Army, the UPA, which had fought both Germans and Russians during the Second World War, issued a defiant call to arms when the Second World War was over. "Wherever you are, in the mines, the forest or the camp, always remain what you have formerly been, remain true Ukrainian, and continue our fight."[103]

Ukrainian nationalism had less appeal in predominantly Russian Stalino, which was now draining its pits and getting its steelworks back into production again. But the town was inevitably affected by the famine that hit the Ukraine, 282,000 dying in 1946 and 520,000 in 1947. Stalin had an indulgent attitude to Khrushchev, on occasions tapping his pipe out on Khrushchev's bald head and chuckling, "It's hollow."[104] But Khrushchev's ambitious plans for 'agrotowns', urban centres in rural areas, made him a convenient scapegoat for the famine – "Spinelessness!" said Stalin and sacked him from his role as Ukrainian First Secretary. He somehow hung on to his job as Ukrainian Premier but was no longer mentioned in the Ukrainian Communist press and his days seemed to be numbered.

The courage of the Red Army and Communist resistance movements in mainland Europe had given the Communist Party considerable status in Wales and Harry Pollitt, the Communist Parliamentary candidate in the Rhondda, was only narrowly defeated in the 1945 election. But, as Gwyn pointed out in his book on Welsh history, "with the onset of the Cold War, and the ambiguous examples of Czechoslovakia and Yugoslavia during 1948, the Communist Party dwindled quite rapidly."[105] Gwyn, by now a student at Aberystwyth, was briefly a Party member but left because he identified strongly with Tito in his battles with the Soviet Union. In the summer of 1948 Gwyn worked with his wife Maria Fernandez as a road builder on the Brotherhood and Unity highway that was intended to unify Yugoslavia. "Tito transcended the multicultural divide in Yugoslavia," he recalled in an interview with *Radical Wales* in 1983, "and stood up to the Russians. I'm still a Titoist."[106]

Hopes of change after the end of the war had dwindled in Ukraine too. There was no sign of the relaxation of repression that many in the Soviet Union had dreamt of. There were major deportation exercises in Moldavia and the Baltic States, as well as in Ukraine, designed to complete the 'Sovietisation' of those populations. And the NKVD even began a new series of arrests targeted at selected ethnic minorities, including Soviet Jews.

Vasily Grossman was horrified at what was happening. He had been active in the Jewish Anti-Fascist Committee during the war but he now saw members of that committee being picked out one by one and taken off to be interrogated and tortured, many in the Lubianka prison in Moscow. Fifteen members of the Committee were put on trial in May 1952, thirteen of whom were later executed.[107]

In order to learn more about the fate of Stalin's victims, my wife Hazel Gower and I visited Our Lady of the Don, the Donskoi monastery in Moscow, in 2007 and were shown around it by a well-informed local teacher. As she pointed out to us, killing on the scale undertaken by the NKVD meant that a huge number of bodies had to be disposed of. Therefore it had taken over one of the few crematoriums then existing in Moscow, that belonging to the Donskoi monastery. The burning and burial of the bodies had then become a mass production operation with the ashes strewn indiscriminately around the monastery grounds.

The beauty of that autumn evening intensified the poignancy of the experience. Little memorials had been set up to particular groups of victims, and flowers crammed in around them. Our guide told us that she had been there one day when two elderly sisters had arrived at one of the memorials with bunches of flowers – "at last we have found our parents' resting place," they told her. It was all our guide could do to contain her emotion. "They killed the best; the rest spawned," were her final words to us.

The dedicated party workers, still struggling to rebuild Stalino, must have begun to have had doubts about the faith to which they had given their whole lives. Certainly Grossman now did and he began work on his great novel *Life and Fate*. In one of the author's disquisitions, he makes what many citizens of the Soviet Union would have considered to be the sacrilegious suggestion that Communism and Fascism were comparable ideologies.

"These call people to carry out any sacrifice, to accept any means, in order to achieve the highest of ends: the future greatness of the motherland, world progress, the future happiness of mankind, of a nation, of a class. One more force co-operated with the life-instinct and the power of great ideologies: terror at the limitless violence of a powerful State, terror at the way murder had become the basis of everyday life. The violence of a totalitarian State is so great as to be no longer a means to an end; it becomes an object of mystical worship or adoration."[108]

Stalin died on 2 March 1953 and the use of forced labour to extend the docks at Mariupol, the nearest port to Donetsk, came to a standstill. Khrushchev, the local boy made bad, moved quickly in the new struggle for power in the Kremlin. Beria, Stalin's executioner in chief, was himself executed, and after a battle for control of the Soviet Union with his main rival Malenkov, Khrushchev came out on top.

As the First Secretary of the Communist Party of the Soviet Union, it was he who took on the job of denouncing his predecessor and the 'cult of personality' that he had fostered. "Stalin, abusing his power more and more," he told the startled members of the Party Congress in 1956, "began to fight eminent Party and Government leaders and to use terroristic methods against honest Soviet people."[109] Some in Ukraine thought that the speech, and the announcement Khrushchev made of an amnesty for some political prisoners, indicated a thaw, and pressed for freedom to debate and experiment.

But they quickly learnt otherwise – it became clear that, even after the amnesty, Ukrainians still made up the largest single group of the millions of political prisoners who remained in the camps. Anna Reid believes that this was because of the Ukrainians anomalous 'younger brother' status within the Soviet Union, "simultaneously extra-privileged and extra-suppressed."[110] Poles and Hungarians were in for even more of a shock: their attempts to liberalise their regimes were abruptly halted and Khrushchev sent in tanks to crush the Hungarian rising.

Khrushchev's speech did cause upsets in the Communist Party in Britain but the South Wales Miners' Federation could not bring themselves to utter a word of condemnation of the Hungarian invasion, even though they did later allow some Hungarian miners to come to Wales to get work in Welsh pits. Gwyn sought some consolation in the Soviet Union's reconciliation with Tito and Yugoslavia and, developing an interest in the writings of the Italian Communist Antonio Gramsci, put his hopes for the future in the more liberal approach of the Italian Communist Party.

Khrushchev made much of his Ukrainian roots,

Gulag prisoners digging the Fergana Canal. Courtesy of: David King

often turning up in Ukrainian peasant costume, and it was he who handed over the Crimea, previously under Russian control, to Ukraine. The Russian-orientated Crimeans claim that he must have been drunk at the time. He did initiate a major housing programme and there are sought-after flats in Stalino for which he was responsible which are still referred to as the Khrushchev flats. But the emphasis of the Soviet system continued to be on prestigious projects like Sputnik, the first satellite in space, and on heavy industry production rather than on the interests of the consumer: "production first, people second – as usual" was how Gwyn summed it up. For the time being at least, the industry that John Hughes had created in the town could continue much as before.

It wasn't long before Khrushchev's thaw began to freeze again. "We were scared, really scared," Khruschev wrote later, "we were afraid that the thaw might unleash a flood, which… could drown us."[111] Attempts to streamline the process of releasing political prisoners from the Gulag were rebuffed by Khrushchev himself and Grossman was in for a shock when he optimistically sent his *Life and Fate*, the outcome of fifteen years work, to an official literary journal.

A year later, two KGB officers turned up at Grossman's home and removed not only his manuscript but also his carbon paper and even his typewriter ribbons. The state censor told him that there was no question of publishing the novel for at least two hundred years. It is especially ironic that one of the most dedicated Communists in the novel – a frontline Commissar – ends up being interrogated in the Lubianka. Grossman died in 1964, believing that his masterpiece would never be published.

But a copy was smuggled out of the Soviet Union and fifteen years later the book at last appeared in print. As another of the novel's characters puts it, "neither fate, nor history, nor the anger of the State, nor the glory or infamy of battle has any power to affect those who call themselves human beings. No, whatever life holds in store – hard-won glory, poverty and despair, or death in a labour camp – they will live as human beings and die as human beings, the same as those who have already perished; and in this alone lies man's eternal and bitter victory over all the grandiose and inhuman forces that ever have been or will be."[112] It was a dream that some in Stalino still managed to hang on to.

CHAPTER EIGHT – NEW TOWN, OLD WAYS

In 1961 Khrushchev decided that the name of the rebuilt town should be changed from Stalino to Donetsk, a reference to the nearby river of Donets, and that it would become the capital of the Donetsk region. There was soon no trace of Stalin in the town, not even in its museum, and propaganda films dropped the now embarrassing name from the past, dreaming of the rebuilt Donetsk as "the jewel of the Donbass region" and a model for the future of the Soviet Union. By the end of the decade, UNESCO backed its claim to have become the cleanest industrial city in the world, despite the fact that its steel works continued to function in the centre of the city.

But the ghost of Stalin had not entirely dispersed. In 1964, Khrushchev was ousted and his successor Leonid Brezhnev not only openly defended Stalin's reputation but also made it clear that Khrushchev's lukewarm thaw was now over. Although Brezhnev was, like Khrushchev, originally from eastern Ukraine, Ukraine was once again made a particular target.

Ukrainian dissidents "saw themselves as conducting a life-and-death 'defensive movement' (*rukh opuru*) against the threat of assimilation to the

Khrushchev became a revolutionary in Hughesovka in 1917, and was ousted as First Secretary in 1964. This image shows him in 1964

Soviet-Russian culture."[113] Ukraine developed the largest national dissident movement in the Soviet Union, mostly based in Kiev and western Ukraine but with a few supporters – including Ivan Dziuba and Vasyl Stus - from Donetsk too.

A new wave of repression began in 1965 with the arrest of two dozen Ukrainian intellectuals. In conditions of secrecy, they were put on trial in Kiev a year later for "Anti Soviet Agitation and Propaganda" and Vyacheslav Chornovil, a young Ukrainian lawyer, was so outraged by what was going on that he prepared a two hundred-page dossier setting out the abuses of the legal system that had occurred during the trial. He was then himself arrested and, says Anne Applebaum, "in this manner, an intellectual and cultural movement, begun by writers and poets, became a human rights movement."[114] This helped to win the sympathy of Russophones in Ukraine and of what Andrew Wilson calls "the highly Sovietised working class."[115]

Information about what was going on in the Soviet Union now spread to the outside world much more readily. The *Chronicle of Current Events*, the house journal of the Soviet dissidents which the newly-created Amnesty organisation helped to disseminate, ensured that it was not possible to claim, as it had been in the 1930s, that Communist sympathisers didn't know what was happening. Not that it had much impact on the South Wales miners organisation – as hundreds more Ukrainians were dispatched to the Gulag, a fraternal delegation was taking banners to Donetsk and claiming that, provided there is peace in the world, "the Soviet Union, from its socialist base, is poised to make a tremendous advance in economic expansion and increased living standards of the people."[116] The delegation seems to have seen little beyond the then thriving coal and steel industry in the town.

But what was happening there did make an impact on Gwyn. By 1965 he had been promoted from Reader in History at York University to a Professorship and found himself in the intensely political atmosphere of a Sixties campus. He became, in the words of Geraint Jenkins, "a popular guru of the new socialist left"[117] and that would not have happened to a defender of the Soviet Union, especially after it had crushed the 'Prague Spring' that had seemed to blossom in 1968. In that year, students at York produced badges enscribed with the words "Viva Gwyn!" and "We are all Welsh History Professors" and his lectures were packed to the doors.

By now, his membership of the Communist Party had lapsed and he was later to say in our film *Hughesovka and the New Russia* that the Soviet Union at this time "began to slump into an organised hypocrisy, with corruption seeping through it like a black slick." In 1970, Donetsk celebrated the centenary of the founding of the city in style but with the appointment of Voldymyr Shcherbytsky, an old crony of Brezhnev's, as Ukraine's party secretary in 1972, repression throughout Ukraine got worse. There were hundreds more arrests of dissidents and the sentences they received were far harsher than those who had been arrested in 1965 – some being sent to the forced labour camps of the Gulag for fifteen years. Shcherbytsky also expelled 37,000 members of the Ukrainian Communist Party and purged half of the Ukrainian politburo.

Alexander Solzhenitsyn, who had himself served time in the Gulag, had been allowed to expose the conditions there in *One Day in the Life of Ivan Denisovitch*, but his subsequent novels had been banned and the concessions that had been made to political prisoners were slowly withdrawn. Frequent and widespread strikes in the camps – and the dissemination of information about them – ensured that they could not be brushed under the carpet by Communists in Britain. Gwyn told me that he had bumped into Mick McGahey, an executive member of the National Union of Mineworkers, on the picket line during the successful miners strike in 1974 and had been urged to re-join the Party. "The Party stinks," Gwyn had told him. "Come in and stink with the rest of us," McGahey had responded.

Yet, in spite of all, Gwyn, like many others on the left, could not discard altogether his belief in the Soviet Union and his hope that one day it would all come right. When he went there in the 70s, it was as if he were on a pilgrimage, stepping on to the deck of the battleship Aurora which had fired the shot that began the revolution and seeing it all again through the romantic haze of John Reed's account. Yet anyone who went to the Soviet Union at that time

Mikhail Gorbachev, appointed General Secretary of the Communist Party of the Soviet Union in March 1985

69

– including myself – knew that your friendly guide was also your minder, ensuring that it was made as difficult as possible for you to hear anything other than the official viewpoint.

And many went with a mindset that didn't want to hear anything too critical. Anne Applebaum rightly identifies a view that "the Soviet Union simply went wrong somehow, but it was not fundamentally wrong in the way that Hitler's Germany was."[118] It was tempting in arguments with right wingers at that time to point to the Soviet health service and the provision of cheap transport – I know I yielded to that temptation myself – as if that excused the continuing barbarism of the Gulag.

Faced with the hunger and work strikes which erupted in the Gulag during the 1970s, the Soviet authorities frequently resorted to the use of solitary confinement in punishment cells, the walls covered with cement bumps and spikes, the floors wet and dirty. Prisoners could be confined there for an offence as trivial as 'sitting on beds in daytime' and although a sentence in the 'cooler' was only supposed to last for fifteen days, the authorities got round it by releasing a prisoner for a few minutes and then putting him back in again. Some prisoners had to endure this for forty eight days at a stretch.

When Professor Emrys Bowen came to research his booklet on Donetsk in the late 1970s, he was less interested in the way that the Soviet Union maintained its control than in reminding Welsh readers about the town's founder and his

technological achievements, pointing out that "we tend to forget the outstanding contributions made in this field by our own people."[119] The contribution that his booklet *John Hughes (Yuzovka)* made to reminding Wales of its connection to the Donbass was important but there was a certain amount of naivety in his approach. He refers to: "the great care and attention that is given to the well-being of the workers whether in the mines or factories or in housing them in the city itself. Working hours at Donetsk consist of a six hour day, five days a week. Since it has been possible to allay the dust problem underground, everything is clean and airy." Perhaps there was a dramatic deterioration after he wrote that but twenty years later the Donetsk miners were to explode with rage about their working and living conditions.

In 1981, when I first met Gwyn, he would probably have shared Emrys Bowen's optimistic view of the way workers were treated in the Soviet Union, a view based on carefully controlled visits. But, two years after the election of Margaret Thatcher and the decisive rejection of devolution, he was in a very pessimistic frame of mind, especially about Wales and Britain. Around this time, according to Geraint Jenkins's pamphlet "The People's Historian: Professor Gwyn A. Williams", "He began to drink heavily, quarrel with colleagues and ill-use even his closest friends and admirers… Deeply at odds with himself, he lived on the brink of self-destruction."[120] Gwyn himself later told me that "I went to pieces, I drank a

Filming *The Dragon Has Two Tongues*, showing author, Gwyn and Wynford Vaughan Thomas. Courtesy of: Mike Harrison

lot, my marriage broke up, I was in a bad state."

Geraint Jenkins thinks that it was the recovery of his Welshness and his television work that "saved Gwyn from oblivion". Certainly by the end of our three years of work together on making the C4/ HTV series on Welsh history *The Dragon Has Two Tongues*, there were few signs of gloom and despair. He joined Plaid Cymru while we were making the

series and had become more optimistic about the possibility of significant change. His fondness for a drink was still there, however, and it was over a lunchtime pint with him in 1985, not long after the miners had been forced back to work, that he told me of his plan to go to the Soviet Union to make a one-man demonstration.

He had just read in his newspaper that President

71

Reagan and Prime Minister Thatcher intended to mark the fourtieth anniversary of the ending of the war with a ceremony on the Normandy beaches – to which the Soviet Union was not invited. But he'd show them; he would go to Leningrad and, if necessary, march down the Nevsky Prospekt on his own. Reagan and Thatcher might have forgotten the twenty million Russians who had died in the fight against Fascism, he told me, but he hadn't.

I told him to hang on before booking his flight while I would try and see if I could get BBC Wales and S4C, the Welsh fourth channel, interested. Both were and, within weeks, Gwyn and I and a film crew from Teliesyn, the co-operative of which most of the team were members, caught an Aeroflot flight to Moscow.

It was a filming expedition that I don't think any member of that team will ever forget. We ran into the usual bureaucratic impediments – our guide insisted on beginning with a guided tour of the Kremlin while we were desperate to start filming – but very soon Gwyn had charmed her into submission. We all seemed to pick up on Gwyn's mood of exultation; undeterred by pouring rain on May Day, he watched excitedly as a huge crowd and mile after mile of red banners poured into Red Square to pass recently selected General Secretary Mikhail Gorbachev, waving on the saluting base where Stalin had once stood. But Stalin's brutal era was long gone, *glasnost* – openness – and *perestroika* – restructuring – were now the key words; perhaps

Communism with a human face was possible after all.

Russians responded warmly to the camaraderie that Gwyn exuded. After Gwyn had told his story of the Russian group playing at his school and sung the *Internationale*, our Leningrad guide said, as we got back into the crew bus, "He is wonderful." Adam Alexander, the sound recordist, shouted to him as he climbed back into the bus, "Gwyn, you've got a secret fan." "No," she responded, "a public fan." And there was a moment when his enthusiastic call of "*Mir! Mir!*" ("Peace! Peace!") to a group of huge war veterans caused them such delight that they picked him up bodily and hugged him.

The climax, both of our visit and of the film that we were making, *Lest Who Forgets?*, was at Leningrad's VE Day anniversary march. Wearing his campaign medals, we hoisted Gwyn up on the base of a lamp post and saw him watch with tears in his eyes as a massed band marched past, playing a tune that for him was synonymous with the courageous Red Army he had so admired as a young man. A bright sun reflected off the brass instruments of the band and, just beyond it, we could see blocks of ice floating down the River Neva, seeming to signify – literally and metaphorically – the end of a long Russian winter.

A year later Gorbachev granted a general pardon to all Soviet political prisoners and soon afterwards he could at last speak openly about what had gone on in the name of Communism: "the lack of proper democratisation of Soviet society was precisely what

Gwyn Williams in Moscow on May Day 1985. Courtesy of: Hazel Gower

made possible both the cult of personality and the violations of the law, arbitrariness, and repressions of the 1930s – to be blunt, crimes based on the abuse of power."[121]

Gwyn and I had by then begun to think of ways in which we could return to the Soviet Union and see that process of democratisation at work. How better than to make programmes on Welsh heroes

73

who had found hope and a dream of a better future
in Russia, men like David Ivon Jones, founder of
the South African Communist Party, Niclas y Glais,
poet and preacher of revolution – and John Hughes,
worker turned capitalist and founder of a company he
decided to call "New Russia".

CHAPTER NINE – SEEING FOR OURSELVES

Gwyn and I did manage to persuade the broadcasters to send us back to the Soviet Union, making *The African from Aberystwyth* for BBC Wales and S4C and including Niclas y Glais in the C4 series *Cracking Up*. Although initially we couldn't seem to stir any interest in Wales about the Hughesovka story, our direct appeal to BBC2 network succeeded. We were naturally delighted, and in the mid winter of 1989, immediately after Gwyn and I had finished filming Niclas Glais in Moscow, we flew down to Donetsk.

The plane dripped condensation, the bread in the in-flight snack was stale and the stewardess had the-customer-is-always-wrong manner that we had got used to in the Soviet Union. By this time the huge hopes invested in Gorbachev had begun to fade a little. The Donbass miners strikes in 1987 made world news when thousands of angry miners marched from their pits, and for five days and nights occupied the square outside the local Communist Party headquarters. And, as Gwyn put it later, "What was the Tonypandy, the Maerdy, the storm centre of the revolt? – Donetsk." Earlier that year there had been elections in the Soviet Union, "the first more or less free vote in the Soviet Union since 1918"[122] according to historian Tony Judt. But this was not a multi-party election and the Communist Party still seemed to be trying to maintain what it claimed was its 'leading role' in the Soviet Union.

Yet Gwyn still hung on to his belief that it would all turn out right. He quoted back to me what our cameraman Ray Orton had said to him in Moscow: Ray was not only a master of his craft but also an always reassuring presence. He had told Gwyn, over prawns and Russian champagne in a Moscow bar, that the change from old style communism to new was bound to be difficult but that it now represented a real hope for the future. In a speech he gave in 1988, Gwyn claimed that "the momentous changes now under way in the Soviet Union will prove momentous for the human race" and spoke of "the struggle to transform the Soviet Union into the genuine federation of socialist republics its creators dreamed of."[123]

On our brief first visit, we saw little to contradict his optimism. Donetsk architecture wasn't inspiring but the city looked clean and well organised. The city took a pride in its poplars, lawns and chestnut groves and claimed that, for its million people, there were a million roses. We were whisked around the sights, with particular emphasis on the historic sites that still survived – the houses where the Welsh workers once lived, the hotel that John Hughes had had built, the walls of part of what was now called the Lenin Steelworks.

We got a very different perspective on the city

Striking miners occupy Donetsk city centre 1987. Courtesy of: Alamy

when we returned to it in 1990 with a film crew. This was to be a Russian/British co-production so half the crew were Russian. Gwyn hit it off with the Russian sound recordist and electrician but soon fell out with Nikolai Kulman, the cameraman. The latter proclaimed himself a Czarist, convinced that only a return to the old regime would restore Russian values. Though good at his job, he was hostile to Communist Donetsk and horrified when Gwyn provocatively described the Museum of Religion and Atheism in Leningrad – then the former Kazan Cathedral – as one of his favourite places in the Soviet Union.

If Nikolai spotted something that would put Donetsk in a negative light – a drunkard asleep on a patch of earth grasping a vodka bottle, for example – he would rush over to film it and this initially encouraged Gwyn and I to find and film positive images about the place. "A beautiful city, broad boulevards, roses bloom," asserted Gwyn in his commentary. But it was becoming clear to me that this wasn't the whole truth about the place and I felt that Gwyn was allowing his romantic attachment to the Soviet Union – and his antagonism to Nicolai's smug interpretation – to cloud his judgement about what we were beginning to see and hear about the city.

Tensions within the crew were heightened by Gwyn's latest attempt to give up smoking: a cloud of smoke would occasionally drift down the table at which we dined together as Gwyn puffed away at a herbal cigarette. Adam and I soon discovered that this was something of a smokescreen, that the nicotine patches he was using were becoming not a substitute for his snatched nicotine cigarette but an addition to it.

One day Gwyn had to manage for five hours with no cigarettes at all. We had arranged to go down a thousand feet at the Gorki pit, one of the twenty-one coal pits within the city limits. It wasn't just nicotine deprivation that led to his assessment of what we saw though: as we filmed our six kilometre journey in a coal dram towards the face, Gwyn's voiceover said, "Above, girdles buckle, the roof bulges, hanging chains threaten to gouge your eye out." We learnt that a week before six men had been killed in the pit next door and were shocked to see men crawling into narrow seams to hack out the coal.

To film them at work, we had no option but to crawl in after them with camera and battery light. Only when I had the soundtrack translated later did I realize that the miner we had filmed was shouting "No oxygen here – call the controller!" Gwyn couldn't continue to ignore the evidence of his own eyes – the commentary he recorded subsequently said, "At the face, men grovel through three foot seams to get at the coal. Four of my uncles and both of my grandfathers worked in some of the worst pits in south Wales. They never had to face this. And Good God! this was supposed to be a workers' state!!"

Gwyn Williams underground. Courtesy of: Adam Alexander

We were invited back to see the miners' living conditions when their shift was over. On the way there I was aware of Gwyn registering some graffiti written up on a wall – Слава КПСС- на чернобыльской земле. He could read the Cyrillic alphabet and had picked up some Russian so he knew what it meant. When we got to miner Vladimir Trofimenko's home, he showed us around, his wife Svetlana pointing out the damp patches. Both Gwyn and I had seen a lot worse but it was a tight squeeze for a family of five and they told us that no matter how long they waited, they never seemed to move up the housing list. Faced with the testimony of a face worker, once the aristocrats of Russian labour, and the direct evidence of what he had seen for himself in the pit, Gwyn was beginning to recognise that something had gone seriously wrong with communist ideals in the Soviet Union.

After we had finished filming, vodka and food were produced and other miners joined us for the round of toasts that so often completed a Soviet occasion – toasts to Wales, to Ukraine, to friendship, to peace. And then Gwyn stood up with his glass raised and spoke aloud the words he had seen painted on the wall. "To the Communist Party of the Soviet Union – on the soil of Chernobyl!" The miners roared their approval and sank their vodkas in one gulp.

It wasn't that the miners were badly paid; indeed when they were paid on time, they were getting twice the average wage. But they had lost all faith in the Party; indeed while we were there, some miners' meetings were discussing whether the Party should be allowed to have any role whatsoever at the pits. "The Party has discredited itself," one miner told us. "It doesn't do anything for the working class now," said another.

Gwyn found this deeply disturbing. "Where does this leave a man like me who once supported this state and despite everything still understands and shares the thinking and feeling that created it in the first place?" While we were in Donetsk a group of descendants of John Hughes and of the Hughesovka workers were visiting the city and he enjoyed chatting and socialising with them. He laughed with the rest of them when, at an official reception, Vincheroff, the recently elected non-Communist mayor teasingly referred to what he called the Hugheses' efforts to increase the local population.

But, as we came to the end of our filming, Gwyn was still struggling for the concluding words that he knew he would have to record before we left Donetsk. His hopes for Communism had been dashed but, whatever our cameraman might say, it certainly hadn't turned him into a defender of capitalism. It was a beautiful autumn evening when Gwyn stood by the side of the city's lake and delivered the following words:

Gwyn Williams after going underground at the Gorki pit. Miner Vladimir Smolyachkov is on the far left, production assistant Siân Gale on the far right, Colin Thomas next to her. Courtesy of: Adam Alexander

The people here come stumbling out of the carapace of Stalinism. They grope after freedom, sufficiency, dignity, while all around gibber black monsters out of Russia's dark past. Many now stampede after the market as their salvation.

The market has been proved an essential. But an unfettered market made an even bigger mess in the Third World than Communism has here. In the 30s the market almost eliminated my people from history. In that time of misery and anger many of us looked towards this place as a life-giving alternative. That was a delusion but now here in their stampede towards the market they are talking about closing every pit in the Donbass. Good God! Is the market going to kill this great city like it killed our coal industry?

Just before we caught our flight home we filmed the beginning of term at a local school. Children gave their teachers gifts of flowers and Gwyn was clearly moved by the simple ceremony that was brought to a conclusion by a little girl ringing the school bell. I think he would have been too choked to deliver a piece to camera at the school on that day but later he recorded these, the final words of the documentary series: "When I look at these kids starting their new school year and the Russia they are growing up in, my stomach turns over. But if there is any hope anywhere, it is here. From these kids will come the people who will build a decent life and a decent society here. God in heaven, they've earned it!"

After we had got back and were halfway through the edit in 1991, we learned that there had been another strike in the Donbass, with a quarter of the pits coming out in support. The strikers were exasperated that the promises to improve pay and working conditions underground that had brought the 1989 strike to an end, were not being fulfilled and they now demanded that control over the pits should be removed from Moscow to the Ukraine. In the turmoil that followed the unsuccessful attempt at a military coup against Gorbachev, the leadership of the Ukraine, after hedging its bets, made a sudden bid for independence. On 24 August 1991, almost every deputy in the Ukrainian parliament voted for an independent Ukraine; the one dissenter was the representative from Donetsk.

As we completed the editing of *Hughesovka and the New Russia*, we decided to include shots of the latest miners strike and of a Ukrainian nationalist rally we had filmed in Donetsk. But it was becoming clear that, although it did not appear to have much support in the predominantly Russian city we had been filming in, a new force, nationalism, was emerging that needed more than token recognition.

That however would have to be the subject of a new documentary and a new chapter. Nationalism and Ukrainian nationalism in particular was to be the theme of a quite different television series – *Blood and Belonging*.

CHAPTER TEN –
BLOOD AND BELONGING

One evening, walking back to our hotel in Donetsk during our preparation of *Hughesovka and the New Russia*, Gwyn and I got into conversation about Puskhin. He told me how Pushkin had developed a kind of dependency on the Czar's censor, who was sometimes the Czar himself. Gwyn suggested that the way that this intensified Pushkin's internal conflicts – proud Russian nationalist but sympathetic to the reform movements hostile to the Czar – may even have contributed positively towards Pushkin's greatness as a writer. It was the starting point for a series idea we developed which we wanted to call *Which Side Are You On?*

Our previous series for Channel 4, *Cracking Up,* had gone down well, *The Times* describing it as "history without the tears", and *The Observer* calling Gwyn "everybody's favourite whacky Marxist wild Welsh historian". A touch patronising, perhaps, but the reviews helped us get the go-ahead for another series presented by Gwyn on Channel 4, which would include the programme we had proposed on Pushkin.

Just before we went back to the Soviet Union in 1991, the old guard of the Communist party tried to overthrow Gorbachev and for a time it looked as though filming there would have to be cancelled. But,

with Yeltsin's help, the coup attempt was defeated and by the autumn Gwyn and I were back in Russia again, aware that the imminent break up of the Soviet Union was stimulating a resurgence of strong Russian nationalist feeling.

In part because we were making a programme about Russia's most venerated poet, we were still getting the kind of generous co-operation that helped both of us to feel that our co-production was something more than a commercial deal, that this was still far from being a ruthlessly capitalist society. One night the local authorities let us close off the Winter Palace Square in Leningrad completely and restage the moment when the statue of the Bronze Horseman of Pushkin's greatest poem leaps off his rostrum and pursues Yevgeni across the Square.

We filmed all night long and then, with one crucial shot still to go, the smoke machine packed in. Almost in despair, I suddenly noticed that all the Russian crew, led by Adam Alexander the producer, were rushing around the Square gathering up twigs and almost anything ignitable. Nothing would be allowed to impede a film that honoured Pushkin. Within minutes, smoke was drifting across the Square and our cameraman Ray Orton got a wonderful shot of the fleeing Yevgeni chased by a sinister figure on horseback, just as dawn was breaking.

But while the film crew and I were out, Gwyn was robbed inside our hotel. It was more of a conning than a mugging, with a couple of Russian men cheerily lifting him in the air while deftly removing his wallet, but he felt humiliated by it and the glow he had had about Russia and Russians faded a little. He had lost some of his zest for life and I sometimes felt that it was as if he were now in mourning for the Soviet Union that he had once believed in so passionately. It was obvious by then that it was breaking up – and that Russians hated the sight of their empire crumbling, especially the departure of Ukraine or The Ukraine as they insisted on calling it.

"Rather than attacking Ukrainians and Ukrainian-ness as inferior… Russians deny their existence," says Anna Reid in *Borderland*, whose title is the literal translation of Ukraine. The Russian attitudes she describes are all too familiar to Welsh people confronted by English jingoists. "Ukrainians are a 'non historical nation', the Ukrainian language a joke dialect, Ukraine itself an 'Atlantis – a legend dreamed up by Kiev intellectuals' in the words of a parliamentary deputy from Donetsk."[124]

Whatever one's attitude to the long suppressed forces that surfaced after the collapse of the Soviet Union in 1991, it was clear that nationalism was once again an important force – and not only in Eastern Europe. BBC Wales decided to make a series on the phenomenon, based on a proposal by Executive Producer Phil George, and I was then brought in as one of the two directors. Gwyn Williams wasn't even in the running as the series presenter; he was now strongly identified with Plaid Cymru, even making a Party Political Broadcast for them on one occasion. The man chosen was Michael Ignatieff, an academic who, by the 1990s, had become a highly respected television presenter, so Gwyn and I would have to adjust to working separately for a couple of years.

Very early on it was agreed that one of the six programmes in the *Blood and Belonging* series would be about Ukraine and that this programme would have to include a sequence in the east of the country. Where better than Donetsk – but this time I would be arriving there not straight from Moscow but after a journey through parts of Ukraine that had seen the change to independence from a new perspective. Most of the Crimean peninsula was as keen on keeping its Russian connection as was Donetsk but Lviv was passionately in favour of Ukrainian nationalism – even the spelling and pronunciation of its name was significant; to the Russian orientated, it was Lvov, to the Ukrainian-orientated, Lviv.

Michael Ignatieff felt the tensions within Ukraine at a personal level. His grandfather had been brought up there, spoke the language and, to the end of his life in exile, sang Ukrainian songs. But Michael confessed, "My difficulty in taking Ukraine seriously goes deeper than just my cosmopolitan suspicion of nationalists everywhere. Somewhere inside, I'm also what Ukrainians would call a Great Russian, and there is just a trace of old Russian disdain for these 'little Russians.'"[125]

At first I had thought Michael a bit of a cold fish; formidably bright – my wife, Hazel Gower, used to call him "planet brain" – he seemed to have little of Gwyn's warmth and passion. But when we visited his grandfather's village, I began to see another side of him, just as he became aware of another view on nationalism. The key moment was when he visited the graves of his ancestors in the village where his great grandfather had been the local squire.

Late in the afternoon, the local Russian Orthodox priest led us down into the crypt and as he lit the icon lamps, one by one, it was possible to make out the granite headstones of his great aunt, his great grandmother and his great grandfather. Just visible in the growing darkness were cuts in the white marble on top of his great grandfather's grave: the crypt had been used as a slaughterhouse in the 1930s and these were the mark of the butcher's knife.

"Nations and graves. Graves and nations," he wrote later. "Land is sacred because it is where your ancestors lie. Ancestors must be remembered because human life is a small and trivial thing without the anchoring of the past… Looking back, I see that time in the crypt as a moment when I began to change, when some element of respect for the national project began to creep into my feelings, when I understood why land and graves matter and why the nations matter which protect both."[126]

There was no hotel or guesthouse where we were – Kroupodernitsa – so we all, including a loudly-snoring sound recordist, had to share a room. Blindly, I had assured the crew that when we got to Donetsk we would be in comfortable hotel accommodation. I had failed to realize that producer Adam Alexander, a master at wheeler-dealing, had indeed arranged for us to be put up in the hotel used

by the upper echelons of the Communist Party. However, by the time I returned in 1992, perhaps because the power of the party had withered away, the posh hotel was no longer available, and we had to make do with the shoddy accommodation we were becoming accustomed to in Ukraine – dim lights, dirty bathrooms, no heat.

To make matters worse, this crew – not my companions from Telieysn but freelancers chosen by the BBC – were not all happy about the filming I had planned in a coal mine . We had an enthusiastic researcher, Lina Pomerantsev, and she had found us a powerful defender of the position of the Russian minority in Ukraine, a burly miner named Vladimir Kolpakov, known to his mates as King Kong. He resolved the issue of filming in his pit for us as he came up at the end of his shift – "Out of the question. Far too dangerous."

So we went back to his flat, much roomier than that of Vladimir Trofimenko, the miner I had visited with Gwyn, but on the eighth floor of a block of flats built by the miners' co-operative. Once again the vodka flowed and Michael subsequently reported the conversation we had with him in his book. "'A box of matches used to cost one copec,' Vladimir says indignantly, 'and now it costs one rouble and fifty copecs. A loaf of bread used to cost twenty-two copecs and now it costs seven roubles. Pensioners have been left to their fate.

'Instead of dealing with these problems,' Vladimir suddenly thunders, 'the nationalists [meaning the Ukrainians] are spending their time in parliament

Michael Ignatieff in the Russian Orthodox church attended by his great grandfather. Courtesy of: BBC

passing laws to change the signs from Russian to Ukrainian and altering the speaking clock on the telephone to Ukrainian.'"[127]

During the making of *Blood and Belonging*, I came to have increasing respect for Michael. The series was about nationalism throughout the world and focused on areas where the issue was especially sensitive – Germany; Serbia and Croatia; Northern Ireland; Quebec; Kurdistan, and Ukraine, the latter three directed by myself. When, in sometimes difficult and dangerous situations – especially during filming with the Kurds in Turkey and Iraq – there were tensions between what was the right course of action and what was best for the television programme, Michael would have no hesitation: our moral obligation to those we interviewed must come first. He felt their pain, realizing how desperate the plight of those nations without a nation state could be.

But his 'planet brain' didn't mean he was able to make totally objective judgements. At the time we were shivering in the Hotel Ukraine in Donetsk, his sympathy with the cause of nationalism was at a very low ebb. "Being a nation means creating your own way of life. What way of life is this?… There is a devastating innocence in nationalists' faith in independence. Freedom itself is never the end of the road – only a beginning."[128]

Much later I learnt that the distinguished Polish journalist Ryszard Kapuscinski had been travelling through Ukraine at about the same time as we had, taking in Donetsk. He was clearly shocked by the impact of raging inflation, having seen a woman in Donetsk selling worn-down cow's hooves. What were they good for, he had asked? "'You can make soup out of them,' she answered, 'there is fat in hooves.'"[129]

He too had picked up the wary attitude to Ukrainian nationalism in the east, for here it had almost been wiped out – "here Russification was more intense and brutal; here Stalin murdered almost an entire intelligentsia." But he was impressed by how in spite of Sovietism and the feeling of having no alternative, that "Ukrainians had kept alive the memory of their first independence, a memory that Bolshevism had tried to erase for seventy years."[130]

Blood and Belonging was a demanding and difficult series, and Gwyn seemed a bit miffed about the amount of time my involvement in the series was taking – and I similarly also felt he was getting on very well without me. He was making a short Welsh history series for Teliesyn with Michele Ryan as the director and continuing his role as an active, sometimes vociferous, member of our co-operative. We didn't let him smoke at meetings so he often used to hover in the corridor outside, puffing away. On one occasion we were wrestling with the problem of how to deal with an absent member who was being difficult. Gwyn leant in through the door and snapped, "In a certain party of which I was a member, we had ways of dealing with people like him – he would be taken outside and shot!"

I knew by then to take his bursts of aggression with a pinch of salt. By now we were close friends.

We both watched from afar but with intense interest what was happening to Ukraine, especially Donetsk, knowing that our chances were remote of going back there again through a television commission. Gwyn's health was deteriorating and, although we had been given the go-ahead for a series on King Arthur and the Arthurian myths for BBC and S4C, it became clear that it would be necessary to keep travel to the minimum.

Gwyn and I always got into arguments about the programmes we worked on, and those about *Excalibur – the Search for Arthur* were sharper than most. We had usually agreed that our history programmes had to show the way in which what has gone before continued to affect us now. But his unhappiness with the present – the collapse of Communism, the apparently endless re-election of Tory governments in Britain – made him want to retreat into the past for this series. Rejecting my arguments, he sent me an angry letter insisting that "I will not accept a subjection of the past to a feeble present in the name of spurious 'relevance'… all that mountainous labouring to produce a contemporary mouse."

Gwyn was by then living in west Wales, myself in Bristol. We met to hammer it out in a restaurant in Cardiff and, by the time we had sunk two bottles of wine and were on to the brandies, had found a mutually satisfactory solution. Perhaps it was the alcohol that did it but, as so often before, we seemed to discover insights together that we would not have found individually. During the making of the series, Gwyn learned that he had cancer. His final piece to camera, recorded by a lakeside in Wales as our King Arthur was rowed away to 'Avalon', did more than make a generalised statement connecting past to present. Gwyn made an explicit connection to his own personal story. Quoting Tennyson, he said: "I prefer to say farewell to Arthur now while he's still recognisable, as Bedevere said farewell on that desolate shore, mourning the true old times that are dead.

Ah! My Lord Arthur, whither shall I go?
Where shall I hide my forehead and my eyes?
For now I see the true old times are dead,
When every morning brought a noble chance,
And every chance brought out a noble knight.[131]

I remember my own youth in the Communist movement and the war when everything seemed possible. A time of hope betrayed, as perhaps all such times are…"

We only made one other programme together. *Gwyn Alf – People's Remembrancer* was ostensibly a seventieth-birthday tribute but we both knew as we were making it that it was going to be his obituary.

Gwyn Williams putting on a brave face as he filmed, at Llangorse lake, the scene that ends the *Excalibur* series.
Courtesy of: Klanger and Bonk

CHAPTER ELEVEN – RETURN JOURNEY

In March 2008, fifteen years after I had last been to Ukraine, I was running along the platform at Kiev, anxiously trying to read the Cyrillic signs so that I could identify the night sleeper to Donetsk. I got on it with two minutes spare, ignored by the three other occupants of the compartment.

But no sooner had the train started to draw out of the station than my fellow travellers gave me the kind of Russian/Ukrainian welcome that I remembered so warmly from the past. A flask of vodka came out, together with four metal drinking cups, bread and an array of meats and I was encouraged to help myself. Despite the fact that I hardly spoke any Russian or Ukrainian nor they much English, we were soon into cup-clinking toasts and discussions on the gains and losses of Ukrainian independence. I tried to buy a round of beers later but one of the three who seemed to speak no English at all then found two words – "No: guest" – and paid for them himself.

The hospitality was very familiar, Donetsk's appearance was not. The city was so transformed that it took me days to get my bearings. Back in the Nineties, I remembered walking down a drab Artyoma Street when a gust of wind caught one of the banners strung across the street – carrying the legend "Soviet Communism Will Triumph" – and sent it sailing past me. Now all those propaganda banners had gone, to be replaced by flashing signs inviting the visitor into casinos, bars and clubs, one unambiguously calling itself "Full Strip".

Stalin had demolished the St. Preobrazhensky cathedral, the city's main Orthodox church; now it has been rebuilt and its glorious choral music, relayed by speakers onto the piazza outside, competed with 'She Loves You' from a nearby club, its name,

St Preobrazhensky cathedral, Donetsk, demolished by Stalin, now rebuilt. Author's own photo

"Liverpool", written in our own Latin script. At the club's entrance there is a life-size statue of the Beatles, with their tracks playing constantly, and when I went to pay my entrance ticket I was surprised to see a large Union Jack behind the counter and smaller versions on the aprons of the waitresses. The music inside the club, played by live bands, seemed more Noughties Ukraine than Sixties Britpop, as did the dress style.

There had been plenty of shops in the Nineties but often the shelves were empty. Now there are stores and supermarkets in abundance; one I went to was crammed with flat-screen televisions and the latest models of a huge range of consumer durables. Some of the furniture and paintings on sale seemed, to my eyes, in execrable taste but the public art on display, especially that in Donetsk's main promenade, Pushkin Boulevard, was a big improvement on the old standard socialist-realist sculpture exemplified by the huge Lenin statue that still dominates the main square.

I witnessed a telling moment in front of that statue. A pro-Russian anti-NATO political meeting was taking place at its base, with about seventy people, mainly middle-aged to elderly and many holding banners or flags, listening to a woman dressed in red. Nearby a wedding party was taking photographs of a young couple, including one of the groom carrying the bride up traffic-heavy Artyoma Street. When they had finished, they walked straight through the meeting's participants and, as the photographer clicked, bride and groom made a mock clenched fist salute, followed almost immediately by the bride giving an emphatic thumbs down. When I returned to the spot an hour or so later, the meeting and the wedding party had departed, leaving only a handful of wreaths at Lenin's feet.

No longer does the steelworks that John Hughes created carry the name of Lenin. It still churns out pollution over the city but it is now called simply the Donetsk Steelworks. There are now five less coalmines than in 1990 and, though Gorki pit which Gwyn and I went down still keeps its old name, it now no longer produces any coal at all: it is kept going in order to help drain out the water that threatens to drown other pits in the area. I tried to get permission to go down again but the manager, ex-miner Ivan Vassilyovitch, wasn't having it – too dangerous, he said. In 2007 there had been a methane explosion in another pit, the Zasyudko pit close by, causing the deaths of over a hundred miners.

On 18 November, a few hours before the disaster, former Olympic gold medallist and local heroine Lilia Podkopayeva, had been competing in the Ukrainian equivalent of *Strictly Come Dancing*. She and her partner had triumphed with a waltz, danced to the song 'Kurgary' which is a much loved Donetsk song about a young man who becomes a miner. Its words were soon to assume a terrible irony:

The heat of the working days
Like the heat of battle
Brought a huge change
In the lad's life.

The Donetsk – formerly the Lenin – Steelworks. Author's own photo

For respected work
For good deeds
The young lad
Strode across the Donetsk plain.

The miners I talked to at Gorki were clear about the reasons for the accident. "It was caused by the fact that no-one cares about people any more, no concern about human life," Sergei Samilyk told me bitterly. "One has to extract coal and that's all that counts – no-one gives a damn about people now." As far as he was concerned, Ukraine was not an independent country – "Everyone cares only for themselves, not for society as a whole." But hadn't freedom of speech helped? "The more you talk, the less people pay attention."

While I was in Donetsk, I tried to find the Welsh banners that had been taken to Donetsk in the Sixties. The Museum of International Connections, where they were once housed, had gone and nobody knew where its contents had been moved. But I did track down a couple of the miners we had filmed with underground eighteen years previously. Vladimir Trofimenko now has to travel into Russia to get work in the pits there, coming back to see his wife and children in Donetsk at weekends. "For those in power," he said, "it's better; for the working man, everything is worse. Flats are falling apart, heating fails and rents are high. There was bribery in the past but now it's expected even in schools and hospitals."

Zasyadko Pit. Foreground: some of the graves of miners killed in the 2007 disaster

Vladimir Smolyachkov was equally critical and, appalled by safety standards: he had got out of the pits altogether. I went to his small flat where he and his family told me how tough life was, while filling the table with all the food and drink they had available and insisting that I tuck in. Vladimir had gone into a small-scale milling business of his own and vividly described the way in which he had tried to adapt to the brutally capitalist society he now found himself in: "Fearing the storm, I grabbed the oars and rowed with all my strength for the shore, rowed until my hands bled. Now at last I make enough to look after my wife and family."

The miners I talked to were middle-aged; did young people see life differently? Their lifestyle had changed markedly since the early nineties, with drinking in the streets, mostly good humoured, and lots of public snogging. The pounding bass made it impossible to sound out young opinion in the Liverpool but I did get a chance in the nearby town of Gorlovka. My guidebook told me that "the country's most unappealing city is inhabited by the nicest people (really!)"[132] and that seems to me to be spot on. Students at the language school there were happy to tell me what they thought about their country in good English and with few apparent inhibitions.

Their parents too told them that life was better when Ukraine was part of the Soviet Union "but they were young and happy then." Another told me that "there was an Iron Curtain then so we couldn't exchange our experiences. Now life is better." Katya Marchenko said that in the past her parents "had constant work, constant salary but now I can say what I want, nobody watches over me."

Most of what they told me, though, was far more negative than positive – "before there wasn't anything to buy," said Vlad Shiryov, "now we have lots of choice but no money to buy." "Today we have nothing at all," chipped in Ivan Romanov, "our parents got free education but now we have to pay." One young woman's last word was telling – "our generation is afraid of fighting for our rights. We have freedom to express our thoughts but it has brought us nothing."

An issue that came up in Gorlovka and in almost every conversation I had during my visit to Ukraine was the relationship between Russians and Ukrainians. Most people in Donestk speak Russian to each other and many feel that the Ukrainian language and culture has been imposed on them since Ukraine became independent. Nadezhda Ryzhikh, a British Council tutor, told me that, while in the past Ukrainians were required to speak and write in Russian, "Now it's vice versa – we are made to do everything in Ukrainian." Maya Sahatska, a fellow tutor, backed her up – "while there are no sharp tensions, those who speak Ukrainian sometimes look down on those who speak Russian."

At the Donetsk museum, I picked up some resentment about the requirement to give only the Ukrainian nationalist version of history. No one now denies that the famine of 1932-3 happened but some feel that the government wants to impose the view that it was part of a campaign of genocide, specifically targeted at the Ukrainian people by Russians. That seems to be the interpretation given on the monument to the victims of the famine that I found in Kiev. The translation there reads, "For the Millions of Ukrainians – Victims of the Famine-Genocide of 1932-3" with, highlighted in red, the words "The emptied Ukrainian villages were filled with settlers from Russia." There have even been proposals that any other interpretation – that, for example, better-off peasants in Russia were just as much victims of Stalinist oppression – should be made illegal in the same way as that of holocaust denial in Germany.

Metal palm tree, Donetsk's symbol.
Author's own photo)

There is also considerable sensitivity about the last war – referred to by pro Russians as 'The Great Patriotic War' and by pro Ukrainians as 'The Second World War'. Liliya Podkopaeva, a teacher at Gorlovka, was disturbed by what she sees as the Ukrainian re-interpretation of that war as one into which Russia dragged Ukraine. Also she found difficult the new tendency to reassess the role of the Organisation of Ukrainian Nationalists (OUN) during the war less as German collaborationists and more as national heroes. As Andrew Wilson says of OUN in his book *The Ukrainians: Unexpected Nation*, "There is no more divisive symbol in modern Ukraine."[133]

The pre-revolution history of Donetsk is safer territory and John Hughes, the epitome of capitalist exploitation during communism, is now honoured by a statue outside the city's new technical college. Unveiled in 2007, he is represented as a curious mixture of worker and capitalist; dressed like a successful Victorian businessman with waistcoat and high collar, one hand holding a workman's hammer resting on an anvil. His face looks visionary as he stares into the distance, as though astonished by the changes in the city he created.

There are other mementoes of him in the city – a John Hughes hotel full of photographs from the Hughesovka period and, oddest of all, two versions of the palm tree that had once adorned the Hughes's grand house. This has now become a symbol of the city, one preserved in a glass pyramid near the football stadium and another – that wouldn't survive vandalism for five minutes in the UK – recently added to an attractive series of sculptures in Pushkin Boulevard.

And those in Donetsk who once thought of John Hughes as an Englishman are now learning to get it right. Walking into the British Council in Donetsk one day, I was startled to see *Croeso i Gymru – Welcome to Wales* on a poster in the entrance hall. It advertised a series of twenty-four seminars, its subjects ranging from "Welsh: the Eighth Wonder" to "Welsh Nation Builders" who apparently include Saint David, Tom Jones, Laura Ashley, Catherine Zeta-Jones and Prince Charles.

The course was over-subscribed and one of the tutors, Maya Sahatska, told me that, when she started preparing for it, all she knew about Wales was "dragons and daffodils". But the seminars, conducted in English, were "like diving into another world… It was as if we were in Wales." During one of her sessions, she told me, the whole group joined hands and sang Bonnie Tyler's *Lost in France* together.

In her part of the course, tutor Nadezhda Ryzhikh drew parallels between the Welsh Not, once worn by pupils caught speaking their native language, and the imposition of Russian on Ukrainians. She also provided the group with an original explanation of the function of love spoons. She claimed it was devised by the fathers of young Welsh women to keep the hands of young Welsh men busy during courting sessions. By the end of the course she had

John Hughes statue, unveiled in 2007. Author's own photo

decided that the Welsh and the Ukrainians are very similar – "We both like music and poetry."

I was, of course, pleased to find my own fascination with Donetsk and the Donbass finding a mirror image in this group of Wales' fans. Before my departure, I made the most of Donetsk's lively cultural life, not only a night at the Liverpool but also an orchestral concert – full-blooded Tchaikovsky – and an innovative jazz session, held in the main concert hall which was packed to the doors.

But I was going to leave Donetsk with a sense of disappointment. One of my train passengers told me that corruption is "the main problem of our country" and almost everyone I talked to agreed that bribery was taken for granted in almost every sphere of life, from traffic police to government contracts. Sergei Samilyk, one of the miners I had talked to, had been soured by his experience of recent years – "Like the politicians, I hang on to whatever I can beg, borrow or steal; I'll give nothing to anyone now," he told me.

This every-man-for-himself attitude expresses itself sometimes in brutal gangsterism. In the Nineties, Donetsk boss and local M. P. Yevhen Shcherban was shot as he got off a plane at Donetsk airport. Shaktor Donetsk manager, Oleksandr Brahin, and his five bodyguards had been murdered at his football stadium and in 2007, Maksin Kurochkin, a 'businessman' with close links to Donetsk, was gunned down as he left a Kiev courtroom. Dimityr Kreynin, head of the board at the Guaranty law firm, frankly acknowledges that Ukraine's judiciary system "is the country's most corrupt branch of power, while the courts are perhaps its most corrupt institutions."[134]

Political analyst Taras Kuzio has written of "the nexus of organised crime, corrupt law-enforcement structures and party officials that thrived in Donetsk"[135] and evidence provided by Transparency International seems to confirm the sordid picture for Ukraine overall – its latest Corruption Perception Index puts the country in 134th place out of 180 (Denmark is at the top, Somali at the bottom).[136]

Throughout my stay I had had the help of a bright and beautiful young interpreter, Ann Guzhvenko, who was a part-time belly dancer. Just before I left, I raised the issue of corruption with her, hoping for reassurance. Instead she outlined her own personal experience of bribery in education. She had had outstandingly good results at school so expected to get one of the thirty per cent free places theoretically available to university students. But it was soon made clear to her ex-miner father that he would have to pay a bribe to get her into Donetsk University and her teacher was told that even if Ann had been Shakespeare, he would still have had to cough up. Her teacher at university had even been told that, despite the fact she was a teacher there, she wouldn't be able to get access to a book she needed unless cash was handed over to the librarian.

I seemed to be encountering the consequences of the "unfettered capitalism" that Gwyn had warned of but do not want to end this book on a despairing

Ann Guzhvenko, interpreter. Author's own photo

note, to make Donetsk's a story of dashed dreams. When we first came to Donetsk, Gwyn was still hopeful that communism could reform itself and even on his last day had hoped that those schoolchildren we filmed would build a decent society there. But now it emerged that we had been filming at the very school that Ann had attended, that perhaps she had actually been among those happy children who ran past the camera. Now I was on the last day of my latest visit to the town, having lunch with one of those children grown into a young woman, a citizen of Donetsk but without any belief that it would be possible to create in her town the decent society that Gwyn had dreamed of.

Ann had given me a present of a CD of some of her favourite songs and translated one that had particular resonance for her:

I'm tired of digging graves just in case
I'm tired of doing Death and Death doing me

sang Sergei Bablein to a surprisingly cheerful tune.

The happiness gone with the wind
Will never return.

She told me how for her that song exemplified the qualities of Russians and Ukrainians, putting up with whatever life throws at you: "What I think of as courage and gaiety when you can see no way out, no hope left."

As we ate, I found myself almost pleading with Ann for a sliver of hope. Yes, I accepted that those who dreamt of fundamental change often helped to produce results that were worse than what had led to the pressure for change. But I have always dreaded the thought that I would eventually follow the well-worn path from youthful optimism to aged pessimism and certainly don't want to end this book on a note of cynicism. Couldn't she think of someone, anyone, in Donetsk who inspired hope?

At first she couldn't and then… oh yes, there is Lilia Podkopayeva. The former Olympic gold medallist from Donetsk had put her fame to good effect, becoming a UN Goodwill Ambassador and founding a charity, the Healthy Generation Foundation, which aims to promote maternal care and children's health. Perhaps that is the best way of dreaming a city, to think neither in terms of changes intended to turn the world upside down nor of a future utopia. But to dream instead of ways of achieving attainable goals, the kind of concrete improvements that Lilia Podkopeva will see in her own lifetime.

I seized on the information about the Healthy Generation Foundation with relief; Ann remained sceptical – "Yes, but I don't like her. Lilia Podkopayeva comes over as so… well…" Earnest? Preachy? Self righteous? "Yes, just so." I felt an uncomfortable flicker of self-recognition.

EPILOGUE

Even though he was receiving treatment for cancer in 1994, Gwyn Williams was still developing ideas for television series. One to which he was particularly committed was *The Lost Tradition* which would have attempted to trace the tributaries of democracy and would have argued that a key part of Marx's teaching had been buried. "To him, democracy was the key," wrote Gwyn in the proposal to Channel 4. "He believed universal suffrage, once achieved, should never be abandoned, whatever happened (contrast Bolshevik practice)."

But it became clear that, even were the proposal to be accepted, Gwyn would never be able to make it. I was filming in Cairo in November 1995 with another presenter when Siân Lloyd, Gwyn Williams's partner, told me on the phone that he was now seriously ill. The next day, my daughter's birthday, I flew home and then went straight on to Drefach Velindre to see him.

Over fifteen years, we had made thirty programmes together. He was almost always a joy to work with. He would prepare and learn his eloquent and witty pieces to camera with care and precision yet retain in them that passion and excitement that made him such a brilliant public orator.

Sometimes he could get very angry – with me, with Wales, with the world. The tensions between my wish to make accessible television programmes and his determination not to over-simplify complex history made for sometimes bitter arguments between the two of us. I vividly remember him, on a train from Paddington to Cardiff, loudly denouncing me for what he saw as my excessive caution over publicising a film on Saunders Lewis, just after Channel 4 had given us the go-ahead. What was the point of writing an article attacking Lewis' anti-Semitism in the small circulation *Planet* magazine, I argued, when in a year's time we would be able to make the same point to a far larger audience. "Cowardly" and "spineless" were some of Gwyn's kinder responses to my advice.

But the next morning he phoned to apologise and his article was never delivered. Over our fourteen years of working together, I moved from hero worship, to affection, to frequent exasperation, and eventually to love.

As my wife and I waited in the long queue at Narbeth crematorium for admission to Gwyn's funeral, we heard the man next to me recalling, in remarkable detail, *Gwyn Alf – People's Remembrancer*, the last programme we had made together, and asserting that Gwyn, not the royal pretender, had been the real Prince of Wales. At the last moment the producer, Michele Ryan, and I had decided not to conclude that programme with the sombre words of Tennyson that had ended the *Excalibur* series:

And I, the last, go forth companionless,
And the days darken around me, and the years,
Among new men, strange faces, other minds.[137]

Instead of ending there, we added his final words about Wales in *The Dragon Has Two Tongues:*

We will live if we act.

That belief in the possibility of building a better world permeated the funeral ceremony. We did sing that sad old Welsh hymn *O Iesu Mawr* but we also sang *The Internationale*.

So comrades, come rally
And the last fight let us face
The Internationale
Unites the human race.

Communism's mangling of that spirit of internationalism had not crushed Gwyn's optimism, though I must admit it dented mine. Twenty years after the founding of Teliesyn, of which Gwyn had been such a doughty member, we decided that the co-operative wasn't getting enough commissions to sustain itself and unanimously agreed that it should be wound up. As an individual freelance, not long afterwards I made a programme that exposed the way in which those Welshman who had heroically volunteered for the International Brigades had been ruthlessly exploited by the Communist Party. Gwyn, with whom I had made a programme venerating the Brigades, would have hated it – as did many on the Welsh left - but I missed the row we would have

had about it almost as much as the feeling of mutual support that we once gave each other. Sometimes in writing this, recalling his sparkling prose, it has felt as if we were reunited, working together again as in the best of the good old days.

I have watched again many of the programmes we made together and re-read much of what he wrote. That process has given me heart. What he wrote in his essay "When was Wales?" is as relevant to Donetsk today as it is to Wales. "Freedom is grounded in the mastery of history. History is more than a word, more than a footnote on a printed page, more than a tired smile in a shadowed study. The corpses of the dead generations do weigh like an Alp on the brains of the living. This is why we must assimilate their experience if only to get shot of them."[138] Gwyn often condensed his point of view into a motto borrowed from Gramsci who had, in turn, borrowed it from Romain Rolland – "Pessimism of the intelligence, optimism of the will."

Just as I was finishing this book, I saw a moving documentary entitled *The English Surgeon* which seemed to make tangible those precepts. The neurosurgeons on whom director Geoffrey Smith focused, Ukrainian Igor Kurilets and British Henry Marsh, are well used to battling with bureaucracies and are all too aware of the way traditions from the past impose on the brains of the living, the assumption that because that is the way things have always been done, that this is how they should continue.

But, undaunted, the work they are doing together in Ukraine is changing one life for the better every time they perform a successful operation. Marsh's concluding line in the programme was "What are we if we don't try to help others? – we're nothing, nothing at all."

Just because it may not be possible to fundamentally change our city, our country, our world, this does not mean that we have to give up on making significant improvements in the here and now. We will live *if we act*.

RUSSIA

Kiev

UKRAINE

Donetsk

Sea of Azov

ENDNOTES

Prologue

1   Sally Alexander et al (ed), *History Workshop* (History Workshop editorial collective, Spring 1975), p2
2   Alexander, *History Workshop*, p146

Chapter One

3   Gwyn Alf Williams, *The Merthyr Rising* (Croom Helm, 1978), p29
4   E. G. Bowen, *John Hughes (Yuzovka)* (University of Wales Press, 1978), p21
5   Theodore H. Friedgut, *Iuzovka and Revolution*, Vol. 1 (Princeton University Press, 1989), p12
6   Theodore Friedgut, "John Hughes of Iuzovka", *Llafur*, Vol. 5 (1991), No. 4, p82
7   Bowen, *John Hughes (Yuzovka)*, p31
8   Susan Edwards, *Hughesovka: A Welsh Enterprise in Imperial Russia* (Glamorgan Record Office, 1992), p16
9   Friedgut, *Iuzovka and Revolution*, Vol 1, p46

Chapter Two

10 "A Welshman in Russia" by Alan Conway. *National Library of Wales Journal*, Vol 9 (1955–56), p302
11 Friedgut, *Iuzovka and Revolution*, Vol 1, p251
12 Friedgut, *Iuzovka and Revolution*, Vol 1, p39
13 Friedgut, *Iuzovka and Revolution*, Vol 1, p47
14 Friedgut, "John Hughes of Iuzovka", p83
15 Friedgut, *Iuzovka and Revolution*, Vol 1, p20
16 Friedgut, *Iuzovka and Revolution*, Vol 1, p49
17 Bowen, *John Hughes (Yuzovka)*, p35
18 Friedgut, *Iuzovka and Revolution*, Vol 1, p55
19 Edwards, *Hughesovka: A Welsh Enterprise in Imperial Russia*, p37
20 *Hughesovka and the New Russia*, Part 1 (BBC2, 1991)
21 Bowen, *John Hughes (Yuzovka)*, p41
22 Friedgut, *Iuzovka and Revolution*, Vol 1, p242
23 Glamorgan Record Office, RMX 6
24 Friedgut, *Iuzovka and Revolution*, Vol 1, p161
25 ibid, p315
26 Friedgut, "John Hughes of Iuzovka", p87
27 ibid

Chapter Three

28 Friedgut, *Iuzovka and Revolution*, Vol 1, p208
29 *A People's Tragedy*, Orlando Figes (Johnathan Cape, 1996), p81
30 Friedgut, *Iuzovka and Revolution*, Vol 1, p201
31 ibid, p144
32 *Hughesovka and the New Russia*, Part 1
33 Edwards, *Hughesovka: A Welsh Enterprise in Imperial Russia*, p54
34 Glamorgan Record Office, DX409/26/1
35 ibid, /5
36 ibid, /7
37 ibid, /12, p9
38 Friedgut, *Iuzovka and Revolution*, Vol 1, p219
39 Friedgut, *Iuzovka and Revolution*, Vol 1, p328
40 Figes, *A People's Tragedy*, p176
41 Friedgut, *Iuzovka and Revolution*, Vol 2, p169

42 Figes, *A People's Tragedy,* p190

43 Friedgut, *Iuzovka and Revolution,* Vol 2, p171

44 ibid, p200

45 Friedgut, *Iuzovka and Revolution,* Vol 1, p281

46 Friedgut, *Iuzovka and Revolution,* Vol 2, p24

47 ibid, p191

48 Edwards, *Hughesovka: A Welsh Enterprise in Imperial Russia,* p64

49 Bowen, *John Hughes (Yuzovka),* p63

50 ibid, p67

Chapter Four

51 Friedgut, *Iuzovka and Revolution,* Vol 2, p229

52 ibid, p228

53 ibid

54 ibid, p261

55 Friedgut, *Iuzovka and Revolution,* Vol 2, p278

56 Figes, *A People's Tragedy,* p465

57 Nikita Khrushchev, *Khrushchev Remembers: The Last Testament* (Andre Deutsch, 1971), p236

58 Glamorgan Record Office D/DX 664/1-5, p7

59 Friedgut, *Iuzovka and Revolution,* Vol 2, p263

60 ibid

61 Simon Sebag Montefiore, *Stalin, the Court of the Red Tsar* (Phoenix 2004), p172

62 Friedgut, *Iuzovka and Revolution,* Vol 2, p328

63 Helen Wareing née Clark, "Growing Up in Russia and Ukraine", *Even the Rain is Different* (Honno), p49

64 Figes, *A People's Tragedy,* p662

65 Wareing, "Growing Up in Russia and Ukraine", p49

66 Voline, *The Unknown Revolution (*Black Rose Books, 1990), pp307-8

67 Friedgut, *Iuzovka and Revolution,* Vol 2, p456

68 Montefiore, *Stalin, the Court of the Red Tsar*

Chapter Five

69 Figes, *A People's Tragedy,* p768

70 Robert Griffiths, *S. O. Davies: A Socialist Faith* (Gomer, 1983), p67

71 Wareing, "Growing Up in Russia and Ukraine", p48

72 Memoir by Helen Wareing, in author's possession, p9

73 *Hughesovka and the New Russia,* Part 2

74 Hiroaki Kuromiya, *Stalin's Industrial Revolution* (Cambridge University Press, 1990), p127

75 Dai Smith and Hywel Francis, *The Fed* (Lawrence and Wishart, 1980), p53

76 Anna Reid, *Borderland (*Phoenix, 1998)

77 Figes, *A People's Tragedy,* p793

78 Margaret Siriol Colley, *More than a Grain of Truth: The Biography of Gareth Richard Vaughan Jones* (privately published, 2005) p85

79 ibid, p225 and 228

80 Reid, *Borderland,* p117

81 Andrew Wilson, *The Ukrainians; Unexpected Nation* (Yale University Press, 2000) p145

82 Reid, *Borderland,* p574

83 Reid, *Borderland,* p137

84 Colley, *More than a Grain of Truth: The Biography of Gareth Richard Vaughan Jones,* p385

85 Gwyn A. Williams, *Fishers of Men: Stories Towards an Autobiography* Gomer Press, 1996) pp19,21

86 ibid

87 Montefiore, *Stalin, the Court of the Red Tsar,* p234

88 Reid, *Borderland,* p121

[89] Anne Applebaum, *Gulag – A History* (Penguin 2004) p104

[90] T. E. Nicholas, *Political Verse* (Niclas Books, 1980) p37

[91] Montefiore, *Stalin, the Court of the Red Tsar*, p319

[92] Williams, *Fishers of Men: Stories Towards an Autobiography*, pp21-22

[93] Wareing, "Growing Up in Russia and Ukraine", p60

Chapter Six

[94] Reid, *Borderland*, p151

[95] Edward Crankshaw (ed), *Krushchev Remembers* (Andre Deutsch, 1997) p129

[96] Reid, *Borderland*, p151

[97] Montefiore, *Stalin, the Court of the Red Tsar*, p389

[98] Vasily Grossman, *Life and Fate* (Harvill, 1995) pp231-2

[99] Vasily Grossman, *A Writer at War* (Vintage Books 2007), pp85-6

[100] Michael Foot, *Aneurin Bevan*, (Gollancz, 1997) p179

[101] Montefiore, *Stalin, the Court of the Red Tsar*, p437

Chapter Seven

[102] Montefiore, *Stalin, the Court of the Red Tsar*, p614

[103] Montefiore, *Stalin, the Court of the Red Tsar*, p278

[104] Montefiore, *Stalin, the Court of the Red Tsar*, p615

[105] Gwyn A. Williams, *When was Wales?* (Black Raven Press, 1985), p271

[106] *Radical Wales*, Winter 1983, pp6-7

[107] Grossman, *A Writer at War*, p347

[108] Grossman, *A Writer at War*, p215

[109] Mark Frankland, *Khrushchev* (Penguin, 1966), p124

[110] Reid, *Borderland*, p205

[111] Applebaum, *Gulag – A History*, p460

[112] Grossman, *A Writer at War*, p862

Chapter Eight

[113] Andrew Wilson, *The Ukrainians; Unexpected Nation* (Yale University Press, 2000), p153

[114] Applebaum, *Gulag – A History*, p477

[115] Wilson, *The Ukrainians; Unexpected Nation*, p154

[116] Report of delegation to the Soviet Union, 29 May-10 June 1969, National Union of Mineworkers (South Wales Area) Minutes, p486

[117] Geraint H. Jenkins, "The People's Historian: Professor Gwyn A. Williams" (University of Wales Centre for Advanced Welsh and Celtic Studies, 1996), p5

[118] Applebaum, *Gulag – A History*, p7

[119] Bowen, *John Hughes (Yuzovka)*, p7

[120] Jenkins, "The People's Historian: Professor Gwyn A. Williams", p9

[121] Applebaum, *Gulag – A History*, p496

Chapter Nine

[122] Tony Judt, *Postwar: A History of Europe since 1945* (Pimlico, 2007)

[123] Gwyn A. Williams, "Popular Front for Perestroika?" *Radical Wales* (1989), p11

Chapter Ten

[124] Reid, *Borderland*, pp64-5

[125] Michael Ignatieff, *Blood and Belonging* (Chatto and Windus, 1993), p81

[126] Ignatieff, *Blood and Belonging*, pp 93-4

[127] Ignatieff, *Blood and Belonging*, p104

[128] Ignatieff, *Blood and Belonging*, p107

[129] Ryszard Kapuscinski, *Imperium* (Granta 2007), p265

[130] Kapuscinski, *Imperium*, p278-280

[131] Alfred Lord Tennyson, "Morte D'Arthur"

Chapter Eleven

[132] Andrew Evans, *Ukraine* (Bradt 2006), p389

[133] Wilson, *The Ukrainians; Unexpected Nation*, p134

[134] *Business Ukraine,* Vol. 2 No. 7, (25 Feb. 2008)

[135] Tom Parfitt, "Killing of Mad Max", *The Observer,* (1 April 2007), p37

[136] www.transparency.org/policy_research/surveys_ indices/cpi/2008

Epilogue

[137] Tennyson, "Morte D'Arthur"

[138] Gwyn A. Williams, *The Welsh in their History* (Croom Helm, 1982), p200

FREE DVD

DVD
VIDEO

Hughesovka &
the new Russia

Best Documentary
BAFTA Cymru

Free DVD with this book!

Hughesovka and the New Russia

Best Documentary BAFTA Cymru, 1991

This three-part TV documentary directed by author Colin Thomas was presented by the late Prof. Gwyn Alf Williams and first broadcast in 1991 as a series of 30-minute programmes on BBC2. The music is by John Hardy, and the producer is Adam Alexander.

Part 1: Hughesovka

Part 2: Stalino

Part 3: Donetsk

"You *will* be interested, I guarantee" David Newnham, **_The Guardian_**

"Breathtaking" **_The Western Mail_**

"Vivid" **_The Evening Standard_**

Also available from Y Lolfa:

£18.95

MICHAEL O'BRIEN
with Greg Lewis

After eleven years in
prison for a crime he
did not commit, O'Brien
reveals the truth about
the CARDIFF NEWSAGENT
MURDER.

yLolfa

The DEATH
of JUSTICE

£9.95

Dreaming a City is just one of a whole range of publications from Y Lolfa. For a full list of books currently in print, send now for your free copy of our new full-colour catalogue. Or visit our website

www.ylolfa.com

for secure on-line ordering.

Talybont Ceredigion Cymru SY24 5HE
e-mail ylolfa@ylolfa.com
website www.ylolfa.com
phone (01970) 832 304
fax 832 782